M000189539

Let's TalkAbout HEAVEN

The Eternal Home of the Christian

Dr. Chuck McGowen

Scripture quotations are taken from the Holy Bible, New International Version®. Copyright © 1973, 1978, 1984 by the International Bible Society. Used by permission of Zondervan Publishing House. The "NIV" and "New International Version" trademarks are registered in the United States Patent and Trademark Office by International Bible Society.

Let's Talk About Heaven: The Eternal Home of the Christian
Copyright ©2001 Dr. Chuck McGowen
All rights reserved

Cover Design by Alpha Advertising
Interior design by Pine Hill Graphics

Packaged by ACW Press
5501 N. 7th Ave., #502
Phoenix, Arizona 85013
www.acwpress.com
The views expressed or implied in this work do not necessarily reflect those of ACW Press. Ultimate design, content, and editorial accuracy of this work is the responsibility of the author(s).

Publisher's Cataloging-in-Publication
(Provided by Quality Books, Inc.)

McGowen, Chuck
    Let's talk about heaven : the eternal home of the
Christian / Chuck McGowen. -- 1st. ed.
    p. cm.
    ISBN: 1-892525-62-3

    1. Heaven--Christianity.   I. Title.

BT846.3.M34 2001   236'.24
                            QBI01-201258

All rights reserved. No part of this book may be reproduced, stored in a retrieval system, or transmitted in any form or by any means–electronic, mechanical, photocopying, recording, or otherwise–without prior permission in writing from the copyright holder except as provided by USA copyright law.

Printed in the United States of America.

Dedicated to my dear wife Kay,
whose beauty, grace, unconditional love,
and friendship, over the past fifty years, have
afforded me a taste of heaven on Earth.

Table of Contents

Part D: "So, What's the Big Deal?"

Foreword

By Two Who Wanted To Know

*O*wning and managing a Christian bookstore for fifteen years, left us little time for any extensive studies of the more intricate theological subjects, such as heaven. However, that all changed in September of 1998, following the tragic crash of Swissair Flight 111 which took the lives of our son Barry, daughter-in-law Julie, and their unborn baby girl. Because they were Christians, we knew that they had gone to heaven. At that point, we needed to learn more of what God's Word revealed concerning the place where our loved ones were spending eternity.

We asked our friend and physician, Dr. Chuck McGowen, to help us. Since becoming a Christian, Chuck has had the gift of teaching the Bible, and he loves to share biblical truth with anyone who will listen, anytime, and anywhere. He seems to have the ability to make difficult spiritual matters appear simple. If you'll merely get Chuck involved in almost any biblical question, the Scriptures will begin to flow as if they had been stored in his mind just waiting to be imparted. Since Chuck's teaching had helped us understand more clearly the details concerning heaven, we in turn were able to share this new information with others. We also had the hope that one day this knowledge could be used to enlighten many more people.

As you read Chuck's book, you will be greatly comforted by understanding that which all Christians will one day experience together in eternity. We would also encourage you to share this new found knowledge with other members of your family and those friends who might be facing death themselves, or who have recently suffered a loss similar to ours.

God has been infinitely gracious to us throughout this tragic experience and we are confident that one day, when we see Jesus face to face, our entire family will be reunited with Barry, Julie, and their baby girl.

To God be the glory!

Sam and Charlotte Colmery

Prologue

"Tell Me About Heaven"

*I*t was a perfectly splendid September morning, and I was rejoicing in its beauty as I drove back home from the hospital. This was Thursday, and I was now retired from the practice of medicine, but Thursday always meant "Visiting Professor Day," and I still had the desire to keep up with the latest information and advancements in the field of internal medicine. Thus, retired or not, I continued to make the Thursday trip to the hospital, part of my routine.

I was listening to the morning news, when it was announced that there had been a plane crash the previous evening. Plane crashes are not all that uncommon, but what caught my attention was the location of the crash site. The reporter related that Swissair flight 111 had gone down in the Atlantic Ocean near Peggy's Cove, Nova Scotia.

It had been exactly one year to the day that my wife Kay and I had stood on that rocky shoal, near the lighthouse at Peggy's Cove. We had looked out upon the gorgeous expanse of St. Margaret's Bay, while a lone bag-piper played "Amazing Grace." Needless to say, it was a moment in time that neither of us will ever forget. But now, as yet unknown to me, there would be another reason to remember that spot and that time.

As soon as I heard the news, I picked up my car phone to call Kay and tell her about the crash. Before I could even get my first words out, Kay told me that she had received a frightening call from our good friends, Charlotte and Sam Colmery, asking for our prayers. Their son and pregnant daughter-in-law might have been aboard Swissair 111.

As soon as I reached home, Kay and I headed for the Colmery's, where Charlotte related the events of the previous eighteen hours.

Their son Barry, a financial planner, was headed for Zurich, Switzerland, where he was to receive an award for his outstanding work as a financial planner. He and Julie had agonized over their decision to make the trip because they would be leaving their two year old twin boys behind for ten days in the care of their four grandparents. They knew that they would miss them terribly; little did they realize, that the ten day separation would be extended for our Lord only knows how long.

On Wednesday evening they had flown from Pittsburgh to New York City in order to connect with Swissair flight 101 to Zurich. However, through some unexplained delay, they were late for their scheduled flight and thus had to be booked on another Swissair departure. There were three additional choices: two flights to Geneva, and one to Zurich. They opted for the earliest of the three, Swissair 111 to Geneva, and the result was disastrous.

None of us knew for sure, that morning, whether or not they had been on the fatal flight. All the Colmerys knew was that Barry had called from New York, the night before, to say that they had missed the first plane, flight 101, but that it was no cause for concern since there were three other flights leaving about forty-five minutes apart. He didn't know at the time which one they would be taking.

I tried all day to get the airline to inform us whether or not Barry and Julie had been listed on the passenger manifest of flight 111. We made calls to the hotel in Garish, Germany, to see if they had checked in there, or if they had called to inform them of a late arrival. We also called the train station in Zurich to see whether or not they had boarded the train that was to take them first to Innsbruck, Austria (They were to vacation there a few days before the Kemper Convention in Zurich). Finally, at long last, around 3 P.M., we got the news. They had been aboard the fatal flight of Swissair 111, and there was no hope for any survivors.

Later that evening, several friends and family members gathered at the Colmery home to comfort and pray with Sam and Charlotte. It was at that time that Charlotte looked at me and said,"Chuck, tell me about heaven."

You see, Charlotte had no doubt about where Barry, Julie, and their unborn granddaughter were at that moment, because that young couple represented two of the most devout Christians that I have ever known. But Charlotte, like so many of us, had not taken the time to study, in depth and, as a matter of first priority, what God has revealed to us in His Word concerning heaven.

Since I had been an avid student and teacher of God's Word for many years, Charlotte thought that I might be able to enlighten her on the subject.

Sadly enough, that was not one area of systematic theology on which I had spent much time. Like Charlotte, I knew "some things" about heaven, but not enough to adequately teach anyone else, or to afford them a sense of comfort. However, I promised her that I would make the study of heaven a top priority in my personal devotion time, and forward her the information very soon.

Within a week, I had given the Colmerys an extensive list of Scriptures on the subject of our eternal home, the third heaven.

Soon after they received it, I got a call from Charlotte, asking if I would be so kind as to lead a private Bible study explaining the Scriptures that I had provided. "I'll do you one better," I said. "Come over to our house, I'll fix dinner for the four of us [a hobby of mine], and then we'll have a time of intense study on what God's Word can tell us about heaven."

After six consecutive Monday evenings of searching the Scriptures together, we all had a better grasp on the subject of heaven. As a result, while still missing their kids more than you'll ever know, both Charlotte and Sam realized that Barry, Julie, and their granddaughter were in a far better place than any of us. They now felt confident that their three loved ones were greatly enjoying God's heaven. Furthermore, they were assured that Barry and Julie were not the least bit conscious of, or worried about, the four of us who had studied God's revealed truth concerning their eternal home, and ours.

Isn't it strange that Christians, like the Colmerys and the McGowens, knowing that one day they would be going to heaven would not have taken the time to learn more about it?

I don't know about you, but whenever I plan a vacation, I learn as much as I can about the place where I am going, what the accommodations will be, and where we'll eat. And these vacations usually last less than two weeks.

We plan the homes that we build. We shop for furniture and appliances. We plan the decor. We "dicker" about the price. We study the blueprints. We really check it all out very thoroughly. And we only live in the house for an average of twenty years or less before we move on.

Yet, when it comes to the place where we will spend eternity, we hardly give it a thought. Maybe it's because we have to die to go there and we don't want to think about that inevitable event. C.S. Lewis observed that "people don't often talk of or think about things they fear, they are just not interested" (*The Quotable Lewis*).

It is for that reason alone that I have written this book. It is for the other Sam and Charlottes: the ones that have lost a son or daughter or an infant child to Sudden Infant Death Syndrome (SIDS); or the Christian that is contemplating his or her imminent death; or the widow that has just buried her husband.

We have this wonderful promise of eternal life, if we have placed our trust in the Lord Jesus Christ and His finished work on the cross of Calvary (I John 5:13). We have this blessed hope of spending all of eternity with our fellow Christians and our Lord. But, aside from "pearly gates" and "streets of gold," we know far too little about it.

The apostle Peter has told us to "always be prepared to give an answer to everyone who asks you to give the reason for the hope that you have" (I Peter 3:15). In order to "give an answer," we need to be prepared. It is my prayer that this humble publication will prepare and enable you to give an answer the next time someone says to you, "Tell me about heaven."

Part A

"Where Is Heaven?"

"Earth, I think, will not be found by anyone to be in the end a very distinct place. I think earth, if chosen instead of Heaven, will turn out to have been, all along, only a region in Hell: and earth, if put second to Heaven, to have been from the beginning a part of Heaven itself."

— C.S. Lewis
The Great Divorce

Chapter
ONE

The First Heaven

*T*he Bible alludes to three heavens, in three separate contexts, but always using the same Greek word, *ouranos.*
They are, in order of increasing distance from Earth, our
atmosphere, outer space, and God's dwelling place, also called
Paradise. The English translators of the Bible used three different English words to fit these respective contexts.

The first heaven they called "air," as in "The birds of the
air come and perch..." (Matthew 13:32). The second heaven
is referred to as the "sky." For example: "The stars will fall
from the sky..." (Mark 13:25). The third heaven is called
"God's throne," as in "...do not swear at all: either by heaven,
for it is God's throne..." (Matthew 5:34).

Before getting into a discussion of the subject of this
chapter, the reader is encouraged to read the footnote in
which we refute a heresy that is being propagated by the
Mormon cult. They have a distorted biblical view of the three
heavens, believing that they are, in essence, representative of
three separate destinies for those who die (see footnote on
the next page).

The first heaven, the "air," is Earth's atmosphere. This is an envelope that surrounds planet Earth. It is divided into three layers: the troposphere (closest to Earth), the stratosphere, and the ionosphere.

The troposphere extends up to a height of ten miles at the equator and five miles at the poles. Its temperature at the uppermost level varies from one hundred degrees Fahrenheit near the equator to fifty degrees in the Polar Regions.

This layer contains the air we breathe (oxygen, nitrogen, carbon dioxide, etc.), as well as dust particles and moisture, some of which is formulated into clouds. It is the only layer that produces weather phenomena; thus most commercial planes cruise at altitudes that supercede the troposphere.

The stratosphere extends out from Earth's surface fifty miles. It is, as mentioned, where planes cruise, and its most distinctive feature is a layer of ozone (O_3). This substance is produced by the action of cosmic radiation upon oxygen molecules (O_2). Its pungent odor can sometimes be appreciated in the air after an electrical storm. Suspended at the thirty mile level, the layer of ozone provides protection against the potentially damaging, ultraviolet rays from the sun.

The third layer of atmosphere is called the ionosphere, so named because of the rich supply of electrically charged molecules (ions) in this region. It extends to a level of three hundred miles, where temperatures can be as high as two thousand degrees Fahrenheit.

These Mormon "heavens" are designated, the celestial, the terrestrial, and the telestial.

The celestial heaven is allegedly the resting place of all "good" Mormons; these would include those people that have met all of the necessary legalistic requirements for celestial life. This heaven can thus be earned through a series of good works. The works consist of adhering to the strictest degrees of law keeping, and other stipulations, set down by the Church of Jesus Christ Of Latter Day Saints—the Mormon church.

The terrestrial heaven is reserved for all the "good people" that have not taken up with the Mormon church or met its endless requirements, but

This first heaven, like the second, which we shall next examine, resulted from God's creative power and genius. In Genesis 1:1, God makes that perfectly clear where we read, "In the beginning God created the heavens and the earth." Note that the word heavens is plural. This would obviously refer only to the first and second heavens, since the third heaven, from which God created the other two, had been in existence from all eternity past.

Genesis 1:6-8 describes the creation of the first heaven. "And God said, 'Let there be an expanse between the waters to separate water from water.' So God made the expanse and separated the water under the expanse from the water above it. And it was so. God called the expanse 'sky.' And there was evening, and there was morning—the second day."

This "expanse," the "sky," is Earth's atmosphere. The water below it is located on Earth's surface. The water above, in the beginning, was a canopy of water vapor that would ultimately come down upon the earth, by way of forty days of torrential rains. This rain, coupled with the breaking up of "springs of the great deep" (Genesis 7:11), a series of subterranean lakes, would ultimately be responsible for the worldwide flood that occurred in the days of Noah.

Thus having looked at the first heaven, we shall now move on to an examination of the second.

---

who have otherwise lived "good" lives. Comprising this group are: Evangelical Christians, other Protestants and Catholics, Muslims, Hindus, Buddhists, Jews, and all other brands of "religious people." Also included, as occupants of the terrestrial heaven, will be those Mormons that didn't measure up to the prerequisites that would have earned them admission to the celestial heaven.

The telestial heaven is reserved for all the "bad" people. The atheists, agnostics, and criminals of every stripe. This they call a "hell," but there is no mention of the wrath of God here, or the eternal fire of which Jesus spoke.

Chapter
TWO

The Second Heaven

*T*he second heaven is more commonly referred to as "outer space," the exploration of which has been the concern of the National Aeronautical and Space Administration (NASA). The searching out of this heaven began when man had achieved the capacity to escape Earth's gravitational field. This was achieved by way of powerful rockets that were able to thrust men and their "payloads" beyond the ionosphere, first merely into an Earth orbit, and subsequently to the moon.

In its relationship to Earth, this heaven is also composed of three separate domains: our solar system, our galaxy (the Milky Way), and the remainder of space.

Our solar system mainly consists of our "star" (the Sun), nine planets that orbit the Sun at various distances, and the satellites that orbit these planets.

In order of increasing distance from the sun, the planets are Mercury, Venus, Earth, Mars, Jupiter, Saturn, Uranus, Neptune, and Pluto. Our satellite is, of course, the Moon.

The only planet within our solar system proven capable of sustaining life is Earth. God has providentially positioned it at exactly the ideal distance from the Sun. A fraction of a percentage point closer, and we humans, along with all other life forms, would be reduced to ashes. That same fraction of the distance further away, and we would all be frozen stiff. In addition to our perfect distance from the Sun, God has seen fit, in His infinite wisdom, to give us just the right mixture of gases in our atmosphere. Too great a concentration of oxygen would cause blindness (this was an unfortunate lesson gained from experiences with early infant incubators); too little oxygen would result in an unbearably thickened blood (low oxygen levels stimulate the production of red blood cells by the bone marrow). Too much carbon dioxide would put us to sleep, and too much carbon monoxide would be incompatible with life.

Our galaxy, the Milky Way, is composed of one hundred billion stars, and its width is one hundred thousand light years. A light year is the distance that an object will travel in one year, at the rate of 186,000 miles per second. Do the math: 186,000(mps) x 60(sec) x 60(mins) x 24(hrs) x 365(days). That number is 5,840,070,400,000, or nearly six trillion miles. Now multiply that by 100,000 and you'll have the width of our galaxy in miles.

If that isn't enough to cause you to stand in awe of the power and majesty of God, consider this: Beyond our galaxy there are more than one billion more galaxies, each containing billions of stars. Furthermore, the "edge" of the universe is now estimated to be fifteen billion light years from planet Earth.

Is it any wonder then that the psalmist David said, "The heavens declare the glory of God; the skies proclaim the work of His hands" (Psalm 19:1)?

This "work of His hands" is revealed to us in many portions of Scripture, but immediately, from the beginning of divine revelation, God makes it perfectly clear who is responsible for the entire universe.

In Genesis 1:14-16 we read of the creation of not only our solar system, but also the attendant components of outer space. "And God said, 'Let there be lights in the expanse of the sky to separate the day from the night, and let them serve as signs to mark seasons and days and years, and let them be lights in the expanse of the sky to give light on the earth.' And it was so. God made two great lights—the greater light, to govern the day and the lesser light to govern the night...."

The "greater light" is the Sun, located ninety three million miles from planet Earth. The "lesser light" is the Moon, which has no intrinsic light of its own, but merely reflects the light from the Sun. The Moon is roughly two hundred thirty thousand miles from Earth, and, as we know, has been the landing place of our astronauts on several occasions.

The above Scripture points out that these two "lights" served not just to differentiate day from night but also to distinguish seasons and years.

The various phases of the Moon mark off the four seasons (Psalm 104:19), and the Earth's rotation around the Sun, determines them. The spin of the Earth accounts for a twenty-four-hour day, and its orbit around the Sun is completed once a year. The Moon, in turn, orbits Earth once every month.

The most amazing statement in Genesis 1:16, is the last: "He also made the stars." It seems almost an afterthought. God merely spoke into existence one billion galaxies, each containing one hundred billion stars.

Job 9:9 informs us that "He is the Maker of the Bear and Orion, the Pleides and the constellations of the South." The "Bear" is Ursa Major, and "Orion" is an arrangement of stars also referred to as "The Hunter."

In Job 38:31-33, God questions Job, "Can you bind the beautiful Pleiades? Can you loose the cords of Orion? Can you bring forth the constellations in their seasons or lead out the Bear with its cubs? Do you know the laws of the heavens...?"

Here, God is telling Job, and us, that He is in charge of keeping the stars in their proper places and that He is the one who determines when and where they can be seen on a clear night.

As magnificent, orderly, and intricate as the first two heavens are, they will not be the place where we believers will spend eternity. Thus, we will now proceed, in the remaining pages of this book, to examine the "third heaven" and our eternal life therein.

Chapter
THREE

The Third Heaven

*T*he only actual biblical reference to the phrase "the third heaven," is found in II Corinthians 12:2, where we read of the apostle Paul's translation up to that place. "I know a man in Christ who fourteen years ago was caught up to the third heaven. Whether it was in the body or out of the body I do not know—-God knows. And I know that this man—-whether in the body or apart from the body I do not know, but God knows—-was caught up to paradise. He heard inexpressible things, things that man is not permitted to tell" (II Corinthians 12:2-4). He begins, "I know a man in Christ...." Rather than boast in the first person, Paul speaks in the third, and tells us that "the man" is a Christian.

The event was fourteen years in the past, and up to that point, Paul had apparently kept the experience to himself—partly out of humility, and partly because the story was so unbelievable.

The phrase "caught up" (the Greek word is *harpazo*) means to snatch or seize. The same word is used in II Thessalonians 4 to describe the rapture of the church to heaven. Etymologically speaking, the English word "harpoon" is derived from it.

Verse two suggests that Paul was unsure about the details of his translation to heaven. He did not know whether he had gone bodily or if it was merely his soul that left the earth; this would be what one might call an extra-corporeal (out-of-body) experience. Since he was uncertain, he left that knowledge to God, and repeated it for emphasis in verse 3.

As an aside, it is worth quoting John Calvin here on the matter of divine mystery. From his book *The Institutes of Christian Religion,* he wrote, "It is unreasonable that man should scrutinize with impunity those things which the Lord has determined to be hidden in Himself." In the same book Calvin also wrote, "As soon as the Lord closes His sacred mouth, we shall also desist from further inquiry." Paul doesn't question the incident, and neither should we.

In verse 4, Paul refers to the third heaven as "paradise." This word needs further explanation.

There have been three distinct places that the Bible has identified as paradise: the Garden of Eden, Abraham's bosom (KJV) or side (NIV), and the third heaven. Theologically speaking, this always indicates a place where the souls of men and women are in a perfect relationship with God.

That was the kind of intimacy which Adam and Eve had enjoyed with God prior to the fall. They had been created sinless and in all respects perfect in body and soul. In the Greek translation of the Old Testament (the Septuagint), Eden, the home of Adam and Eve prior to the fall, is called "paradise."

The next reference to the word "paradise" is found in Luke 23:43, where Jesus assures the newly converted thief on the cross that, "today you will be with me in paradise." That would be the place referred to in Luke 16:22 as Abraham's side (bosom). This was a portion of the grave where believing souls had departed to await Christ's own resurrection from the grave. When Jesus died, He descended to this place and ultimately took those elect souls to the third heaven.

23

People such as Adam, Eve, Abel, Noah, Abraham, the patriarchs, the prophets, King David, Job, John the Baptist, and many other Old Testament saints, would have been there awaiting their final redemption.

Job spoke of this redemption in Job 19:25-27: "I know that my Redeemer lives, and that in the end He will stand upon the earth. After my skin has been destroyed, yet in my flesh I will see God; I myself will see Him with my own eyes— I, and not another. How my heart yearns within me!"

That is an amazing statement, when you consider the fact that Job uttered those words over eleven hundred years before Christ's first advent, while Christ was still living in heaven with the Father and the Holy Spirit. Job also had the faith to believe that, even though he would taste physical death, he would one day be in the third heaven and see God face to face.

The final reference to "paradise," is found in Revelation 2:7, where the "tree of life" is mentioned as being located in "the paradise of God." As we will see in chapter eight, the tree of life is located in the third heaven.

While Paul was in the third heaven, he heard some amazing things—things that are not for us to know until we get there. These are things which we mortals, in our finite states, could never possibly comprehend.

In Deuteronomy 26:15, Moses calls the third heaven God's "holy dwelling place." In Revelation 4:1, the apostle John, living in exile on the Isle of Patmos, tells of his personal vision of the third heaven. "After this I looked, and there before me was a door standing open in heaven." In verse 2, he reports seeing "a throne...with someone sitting on it." In verse 8, he describes some angelic beings that "never stop saying: Holy, Holy, Holy, is the Lord God Almighty."

You will note that these angels repeated the word "Holy" three times. In Jewish culture this automatically elevated the adjective to the level of the superlative; repeating a word or phrase twice always stressed the point being made in a comparative sense.

Of all God's attributes, only His holiness is stated in such an emphatic way. Neither His love, grace, goodness, mercy, justice, power, wisdom, immutability, ubiquity, sovereignty, nor any of His other attributes are ever spoken of in the superlative. It's not that these are any less infinite or important; rather, God's holiness is the basis, or the foundation, upon which all of His character rests.

Yes, God is holy, and thus, heaven by necessity must also be holy or God would not—could not—dwell there. There is no place for sin or a sinner in heaven. The prophet Habakkuk said to God, "Your eyes are too pure to look on evil..." (Habakkuk 1:13).

Only those deemed righteous and holy, by faith in Christ, and who have thus been clothed in the righteousness of Christ, are permitted to dwell with God there. (More on this in Chapter Five.)

When the chief angel (Lucifer) sinned, God cast him out of heaven and with him all of those angels who had followed his lead. The account of this cosmic rebellion is found in two places; Isaiah 14:12-15 and Ezekiel 28:14-17. I encourage you to read these passages in their entirety.

In the Ezekiel reference we read, "...I drove you in disgrace from the mount of God, and I expelled you...." It also says, "...I threw you to the earth...." Thus Satan (also called Lucifer and the Devil) has roamed the earth ever since, and has been in charge of millions of fallen angels (demons) who do his bidding.

As an aside, C.S. Lewis, in his book *The Screwtape Letters*, said that Christians make one of two mistakes when it comes to the subject of Satan: one, they deny his existence, or two, they blame him for everything that is bad.

It was from the third heaven, that God created the other two heavens. Of course when we say "God," the creator, we are speaking of Him in the trinitarian sense. He is one in essence, yet three in person: Father, Son, and Holy Spirit.

The Son, Jesus Christ, also called the Word, was the agent, or instrumental cause, of creation. "Through Him all things were made: without Him nothing was made that has been made" (John 1:3). In Hebrews 1:2 we read that the Son "made the universe," and in Colossians 1:16, Paul's tells us that, "...by him all things were created: things in heaven and on earth, visible and invisible...."

In the creation narrative, of Genesis chapter one, the Holy Spirit is mentioned as "hovering over the waters" (verse 2).

In Genesis 1:26, the use of plural personal pronouns points to the Trinity. There we read of God saying, "Let *us* make man in *our* image..." (emphasis added).

While it is true that God's dwelling place has always been, and always will be, the third heaven, the Bible also speaks of Him as being in the other two heavens as well. This relates to His divine attribute of omnipresence, or ubiquity.

King Solomon made mention of this particular attribute in I Kings 8:27, "But will God really dwell on earth? The heavens, even the highest heaven, cannot contain you. How much less this temple I have built." The "heavens" that Solomon refers to are numbers one and two, while the "highest heaven" is the third—paradise.

In Jeremiah 23:23-24, God proposes three questions, relating to His ubiquity: "Am I only a God nearby...and not a God far away?" "Can anyone hide in secret places so that I cannot see him?" "Do not I fill heaven and earth?"

Thus, while God's dwelling place is in the third heaven, where He has set His "glory above the heavens" (Psalm 8:1), He also permeates and fills the other two. God's dwelling above the universe is spoken of, theologically, as his "transcendence," while His nearness to us on earth is referred to as His "immanence."

I'm sure that the question, "Where is heaven?" has been asked by countless numbers of people since the beginning of time. But I remember quite vividly a specific occasion when it was asked by one of our local talk radio hosts, whom we will refer to as Joe (not his real name). He had as his guest that day the bishop of the local Catholic diocese.

In a most sincere tone of voice, Joe asked the bishop, "Your Excellency, where is heaven?" What I heard next was appalling. I could hardly believe my ears. The bishop actually answered, "Heaven is not a place."

How was it possible that the spiritual leader of the largest Christian denomination in our valley did not know that the Bible specifically teaches that heaven *is* a place? Furthermore, I pondered, "If he is unaware of this truth, how many other biblical truths have escaped his ken?"

Apparently the program engineer on this radio station, whom I know to be Christian, was equally dismayed, for he promptly displayed the following question on the window that separated himself from Joe and the bishop: "What about John 14:2?" That Scripture reads, "In my Father's house are many rooms.... I am going there to prepare a place for you."

That verse clearly states that heaven ("My Father's house," i.e., dwelling place) is a specific *place*. Furthermore it says, quite clearly, that Jesus is going there. In verse 3 Jesus says, "And if I go and prepare a place for you, I will come back and take you to be with me that you also may be where I am."

In other words, Jesus is going to a *specific place*, to prepare a *particular place* for us (the Christians), so that He can come to the *exact place* where we are when we die, and then take us to the *special place* that He has prepared for us. And all of this activity, on the part of Jesus, is performed so that we can *be with Him* in that *definite place* forever.

It doesn't get much clearer that that!

When Joe pointed out the message on the window, the bishop made another equally appalling statement, "Oh, in that verse, the word 'place' is used as a metaphor. Jesus often used a great many metaphors in the course of His teachings."

While it is true that Jesus often spoke in metaphors, as in, "The kingdom of God is like...," even so, He didn't say that here. He didn't say, "My destination and yours is 'like' a place, but it's not really a place." And furthermore, He didn't refer to His Father's dwelling as "like"a place.

I really felt sorry Joe. He had asked his bishop, his spiritual guide, a very sincere spiritual question, and all he got was an evasive—and, I might add, heretical—answer. Thus, I sent Joe a copy of all of the scriptural references that I had collected for Sam and Charlotte Colmery. I hope that Joe now realizes that heaven is a place, and I hope that he finally has a better understanding of where it is.

We have not been given the whole story on heaven. It's too comprehensive and unfathomable for our meagerly finite minds to grasp. But we have been given a great deal of information on which to base our blessed hope of eternal life. It's what the apostle Paul called "faith and knowledge resting on the hope of eternal life" (Titus 1:2).

With that in mind, we can now proceed to Part B to discover what heaven will be like and just what we believers can look forward to in that beautiful "place" prepared for us "since the creation of the world" (Matthew 25:35).

Part B

"What Will Heaven Be Like?"

"No eye has seen, no ear has heard, no mind has conceived what God has prepared for those who love Him."

— I Corinthians 2:9

Chapter
FOUR

The Eternal Heaven

*J*t should come as no surprise that we mortals have such a difficult time understanding the concept of eternity. After all, we are finite, and eternity is, by definition, infinite. The finite can never fully comprehend the infinite. If you doubt that, consider this: if you divide infinity by two, you still have infinity.

The *World Book Dictionary* defines infinite as being "without limits; endless; boundless: greater than any assignable quantity or magnitude." Yet, the Bible tells us that we still have a secret longing for the eternal—an eternity that we don't even understand. Solomon confirms this as he writes in Ecclesiastes 3:11 that God has "...set eternity in the hearts of men; yet they cannot fathom what God has done from the beginning to the end."

In other words, how can we understand this concept of an eternal, infinite existence, when we can't even "fathom" God's activities within a time frame? It is a frame referred to as "the beginning to the end." Those divine activities would include His acts of creation and His control of the material universe, which, like us, is finite.

The apostle Paul states in II Corinthians 4:18 that "...What is seen is temporary, but what is unseen is eternal." The third heaven is part of that "unseen" which is eternal.

Time is an issue with which God does not concern Himself. Time was established by God for the benefit of His creatures. Peter reminds us that "...with the Lord a day is like a thousand years, and a thousand years are like a day" (II Peter 3:8).

In other words, time is a reference point for us, but not for God. We need time to maintain a sense of orientation. Without an awareness of the clock or the calendar, we tend to become confused, disoriented.

I can best illustrate this fact by the concept of the vertical. Being upright creatures that walk on two legs, we are naturally oriented to the vertical (although I know a few "couch potatoes" who seem more compatible with a horizontal position).

Some of you may remember a place in the old amusement parks called the "Fun House." There was always one room there where all the walls were slanted, the pictures were nailed to the wall in a similar slant, and the furniture was tilted in the same manner. All reference angles were about ten degrees off the absolute vertical of ninety degrees. As soon as you entered the room, you had a tendency to lean in the direction of the slant, even though your feet were on a perfectly level floor. In other words, you tried to orient your body in the direction of that which you thought was vertical. Because of the fact that the assumed "vertical" was really at eighty degrees in relation to the floor (instead of ninety degrees), you leaned toward the eighty degrees so as to "right" yourself.

So it is with time. We use watches, calendars, daylight and night to "right" ourselves into a proper time frame.

In hospital intensive care units, where people are acutely ill, there is always a tendency toward disorientation. This used to be potentiated by a lack of windows, clocks, and calendars. Now, through experience, we have learned to replace those missing items and enable people to maintain some semblance of time orientation.

In spite of the fact that God has "set eternity" in our hearts, we remain secular beings. The word "secular" has taken on a rather pejorative context in the Christian community, mainly due to its association with "secular humanism."

The word secular comes from the Latin word *saeculum*, meaning age or span of time, the world of time. To be secular is not a bad thing, it's inevitable and perfectly natural. To be a "secularist" however, means that one believes *only* in this world of time but not in eternity, and that is a bad thing.

One of the twentieth century's most notorious secularists was the late Carl Sagan. During his popular PBS program "Cosmos," he was often heard to say, "The cosmos, the cosmos. It is all that is, ever was, or ever will be." *Cosmos* is another Latin word that refers to the world order or system. Sagan used the term as synonymous with the universe.

Sagan died a few years ago and, by now, has undoubtedly learned that he was wrong. His soul continues to live on, outside of the cosmos, either in hell, because of his unbelief, or in heaven, if he hopefully made a last minute, deathbed commitment to the truth of Jesus Christ.

Time is the essence of earthly life, but in heaven, time as we know it, will not exist. Ecclesiastes 3:1 reads, "There is a time for everything, and a season for every activity under heaven." All of our activities "under heaven"—in other words, on earth—are time oriented. We live by schedules. We make appointments. We wear watches, hang calendars, and plant or reap according to the season.

In the Shakespearean play *Hamlet*; there is that notorious line, "To be or not to be? that is the question." This assertion by Hamlet arose when he had discovered that his mother and uncle, who were lovers, had plotted the murder of his late father. This discovery so troubled Hamlet that he became severely depressed and was thus contemplating suicide. This prompted his famous question, "To be or not to be?"

This however, was a totally fallacious statement. It was based upon the erroneous premise that when one dies, one ceases *to be*. It is instead, axiomatic that once one "becomes," one will always "be." From the time of conception, when a human sperm penetrates a human egg, and that first combined component of DNA (one half from the father and one half from the mother) exists in the first human cell, God places a soul there, and we have "become."

David admits, in Psalm 51:5 that he was "sinful from the time my mother conceived me." It is the soul that possesses this original sin. Thus David acknowledges that his soul was present at conception. We will discuss the soul in greater detail in Chapter Seventeen.

Therefore, in regard to our "being," the question that Hamlet should have raised—and one that all people should contemplate—is not "whether to be" but "where to be." The answer to that question depends on what a person has done with his or her knowledge of the Lord Jesus Christ. Is He Lord and Savior, truly God, Sovereign of the universe and one person of the Trinity, or merely a historical figure who said some nice things, set a good example for living and died a martyr's death?

In heaven, we will have slipped the bonds of time, for we, like God and His heaven, will be eternal. When the shuttle Challenger exploded, killing all on board, President Ronald Reagan repeated a famous quotation and said that; "they have slipped the bonds of Earth to touch the face of God." The "bonds" that the president referred to were those of both gravity and time.

One of the many names for God, and one that implies His eternality, is the Hebrew word *Yahweh* (in English "Jehovah"). It means, I Am, and is written LORD in English translations of the Bible. Signified in large case letters, this is meant to distinguish that name and person of God the Father, from God the Son, whose name is written Lord in the Old Testament. The Hebrew word here is *Adonai*. Psalm 110:1 reads, "The

LORD said to my Lord; sit at my right hand…." This means literally that *Yahweh* said to *Adonai*, or the Father said to the Son, "sit at my right hand."

God calls Himself, "I Am." He does not say, "I was" or "I will be." Those imply change and a time based orientation. He is always the same. He is immutable; He is changeless. He is always in the present. He is neither in the past nor the future, for those are time-oriented references.

In Psalm 39:5, David says to God, "You have made my days a mere hand breadth; the span of my years is nothing before you. Each man's life is but a breath." Here, David was comparing his life on Earth, which by human standards was long (I Chronicles 29:28), to eternity and to God's eternal existence and perspective.

When someone that we now miss (because they went to be with Christ some time ago) meets us in heaven, their conversation won't begin, "I've been waiting such a long time to welcome you into our eternal home in heaven." They won't even be aware of the hiatus of time between their "going home" and ours. The conversation is more apt to begin,"now as I was saying before we were interrupted…."

The last verse of John Newton's great hymn, "Amazing Grace," reads, "When we've been there ten thousand years, bright shining as the Sun, we've no less days to sing God's praise than when we first begun." Newton obviously possessed an eternal perspective. Eternity or infinity, minus ten thousand still equals eternity! I John 5:1-12 reads, "God has given us eternal life, and this life is in His Son. He who has the Son has life."

Now I ask you, "do you have the Son?"

Chapter FIVE

The Residents
of Heaven

When we get to heaven, who will be there with us? The short answer is the Creator and many of His creatures. The long answer is much more complex.

As stated earlier, the Creator is one in essence yet three in person: the Father, the Son and the Holy Spirit. This trinity, though never mentioned as such in the Bible, is implied in many places. One of those is found in Matthew 28:19 where Jesus told His disciples to baptize new believers in the *name* (singular) of the Father, Son, and Holy Spirit. The use of the singular word "name" implies the one essence. The naming of the three persons of the Godhead confirms a plurality of persons.

There was a "time" (I don't know how else to say it) when the eternal heaven was occupied exclusively by these three. They have always been there—with the exception of the thirty-three years that Jesus lived on the earth—and they have been conversing with and loving each other from eternity past.

I once heard a preacher say that God created man so that He would have someone to love, because love always needs an object. While it is true that love does need an object, it is not true that God needed us to love. God the Father had the Son and the Spirit, and they in turn had each of the other two to love. In addition to that fact, to say that God needs anything is to be grossly ignorant—if not heretical—of God's attributes. God is utterly self-sufficient; he has no needs apart from Himself. The apostle Paul reminds us of this fact in Acts 17:25, where he says, "He is not served by human hands, as if He needed anything...."

In addition, the persons of the trinity have always conversed with one another. We see evidence of that in Genesis 1:26, where one person of the Godhead says to the other two, "Let *us* make man in *our* image" (emphasis added). In Genesis 3:22 the one speaks and says to the other two, "The man has now become like *us*..." (emphasis added). Then again, in Genesis 11:7, the conversation continues, "Come let *us* go down and confuse their language" (emphasis added).

The first of God's creatures were the angels. In speaking to Lucifer, the initial one of many angels to fall, that is to sin against the Creator, God said, "You were blameless in your ways from the day you were created, till wickedness was found in you" (Ezekiel 28:15).

God had made millions of angels (Psalm 68:17). They were made both to serve Him (Psalm 103:120-121) and to guard all current believers, as well as those of the past and all who will one day become believers (Hebrews 1:14).

Angels were present and watching while God created the universe (Job 38:4-7). The faithful ones will be with God, and us, serving and praising Him forever (Revelation 5:11-12).

However, not all of the millions of created angels will share eternity with us in heaven. Millions fell when they chose to follow Satan, and they will eventually burn with him in the eternal fires of damnation along with all unbelievers (Matthew 26:41)

Last, but certainly not least, God's elect, His chosen ones, will occupy heaven. In heaven there is a place prepared for us (see I Corinthians 2:9; John 14:2; Matthew 25:34).

Who are these elect? They are believers whom God, in His sovereign will and for His own pleasure and purpose, chose, even before He created the universe (Ephesians 1:4-5,11). These are people that have been appointed for eternal life (Acts 13:48; I Thessalonians 5:9). They are people who have trusted in God's Word and the atoning work of His Son, Jesus Christ, who died on the cross for their sins. Based upon that trust, they have been given eternal life. These are people that have been awakened by God from the "deadness" of their sin (Ephesians 2:5), have recognized their sinful state, have repented of that sin, and have asked for God's forgiveness.

Jesus calls the elect His sheep. John 10:27-28 reads, "My sheep listen to my voice; I know them and they follow me. I give them eternal life, and they shall never perish; no one can snatch them out of my hand."

In I John 5:13 we read, "These things I write to you who believe in the name of the Son of God so that you may know that you have eternal life."

What does it mean to believe? There are three Latin words for believing, each denoting a separate level of belief. Each level is a pre-requisite to the next.

The first is *noticia*. This means to "note" the facts; be aware of them. Paul asks in Romans 10:14, "How can they believe in the one of whom they have not heard?" In order to believe in Jesus, one must have first heard the facts about Him. Believing *about* Jesus is a level where many people find themselves. They know the facts about Him. They've heard it said that He claimed to be divine; that He was born of a miraculous virgin birth; that He lived a perfectly sinless life; that He died on a cross for our sins; and that He subsequently arose from the dead. Finally, they have heard that, having gone back to heaven, Jesus promised to one day return.

They have "heard" with their ears but not necessarily their hearts. They have not accepted the facts as being true. This type of "belief," *noticia*, does not result in any change in their lives because they are still spiritually dead (Ephesians 2:1-2). This type of "faith" is not saving faith (James 2:17).

Still, this level, while not representing true faith, is a necessary prerequisite to attaining the next. To move to the subsequent level however, requires an act of God's saving grace, wherein we are enabled to accept the facts noted at the first level (see II Corinthians 4:6; John 6:65).

When we assent to the verity of the facts concerning Christ, we are displaying the second level of faith: *assensus*. This is the level of knowledge possessed by a newly, spiritually reborn, child of God (John 3:3).

With growth, through a study of the Word of God and the sanctifying work of the Holy Spirit in renewing our minds (Romans 12:2), we ultimately attain the third level of belief: *fiducia*, meaning trust. In Proverbs 2:1-6 we read, "My son, if you accept my words and store up my commands within you, turning your ear to wisdom and applying your heart to understanding, and if you call out for insight and cry aloud for understanding, and if you search for it as a hidden treasure, then you will understand the fear of the LORD and find the knowledge of God." The more we know God and the more we comprehend His many attributes, the more we will trust in Him and display the ultimate level of belief: *fiducia*, or trust.

In the world of finance there are trusts. These are financial instruments where people place their assets to protect them from confiscatory taxation when they die (the inheritance tax). The manager of the trust is called a fiduciary—one in whom a person places their trust to manage the trust.

By growing and trusting God more and more, this fiducial trust grows too. Unfortunately, too many of we Christians have not grown sufficiently to attain a perfect trust. Proverbs 3:5 tells us to "Trust in the Lord with *all* your heart." The verse goes on to say that we should not lean on, or trust in, our own understanding of things—especially things of God. Too often our "understanding" is based on fiction not fact, and tradition rather than biblical truth.

Matthew 25:31-46 speaks of two kinds of destinies, using metaphors for two kinds of people. The first kind of people, the unbelievers, are called goats (it is no coincidence that a goat head is a common logo used by satanic cults). The other kind of people are referred to as sheep. These are the elect, the believers, the chosen ones of God.

This passage tells us that the goats are placed on the left and the sheep on the right (verse 35). Verse 41 says that the destiny of those on the left, the goats, is "eternal fire prepared for the devil and his angels."

The destiny of those on the right, the sheep, those with either an assensus or a fiducia level of faith is "eternal life" (verse 46).

Another term for a believer is, one who has been "saved." This is a term that is frequently used but seldom understood. We often hear Christians ask people the question, "Are you saved?" The next time you hear that, ask the questioner another question: "Saved from what?" Very often they're stuck for an answer.

Here is the answer they ought to give. "We are saved from God's wrath." I Thessalonians 5:9 reads, "For God did not appoint us to suffer wrath but to receive salvation through our Lord Jesus Christ."

We hear a great deal these days about God's love, but very little about His wrath. There is a tendency among many clergy to shy away from the "fire and brimstone" sermons of days gone by. Few realize that Jesus spoke twice as often on the subject of hell as He did on heaven. Hell is a place of eternal fire, punishment, and damnation that has no end. It's a place where the consummate wrath of God is meted out to the unbelievers of all time.

But we, as believers have been saved from that wrath. I Thessalonians 5:9, cited above, assures us of that.

There are many other names, or designations, scattered throughout the Bible,that refer to the eternal human residents of heaven. These include: the elect, the remnant, the bride of Christ, the way, the redeemed, the children of God, God's chosen people, a royal priesthood, the body of Christ, a holy nation, saints, Christians, and the church.

The *elect* are those people whom God chose (elected) to spend eternity with Him. We didn't elect Him, He elected us (Romans 9:11-12). He did this "...not because of anything we have done but because of His own purpose and grace" (II Timothy 1:9).

The *remnant* (Romans 11:5) refers to true, or spiritual, Israelites. These are either Jews of the Old Testament who have trusted in what Christ would do in the future (John 8:56), or those who, since the death of Christ, have trusted in what He has done in the past regarding their salvation (I Peter 2:24).

We believers are collectively called the *bride of Christ* because we will be married to Jesus in heaven (Revelation 19:7). This relationship will replace the marital relationship which couples have on earth (Luke 20:34-35). We will explain this further in Chapter Fourteen.

Followers of Christ in the first century often referred to themselves as *the way* (Acts 9:1-2; 24:14). This was presumably because Jesus had told them that He was the only "way" by which they could approach God (John 14:6).

The elect are also called the *redeemed* (I Peter 1:18) and Christ is our Redeemer (Galatians 3:13; Job 19:25).

Believers are called *children of God* (I John 3:1) because they have been adopted into the family of God. This occurs by way of a miraculous re-birth which God initiates (John 1:12-13), following which we receive Christ by faith. Regeneration precedes faith.

The designation *chosen* relates to the fact that God decided long before we were born, even before He created the universe, that he wanted us to live with Him eternally. This decision was His alone and was not based on any innate worth that He saw in us (II Timothy 1:9). God's sovereign choice was entirely unmeritable, as far as we are concerned, and is thus referred to as "grace." Ephesians 1:4-5 gives the best biblical illustration of God's decision concerning our salvation: "For He chose us in Him before the creation of the world to be holy and blameless in His sight. In love He predestined us to be adopted as His sons through Jesus Christ, in accordance with His pleasure and will."

We are called a *royal priesthood* because, as believers, we are to fulfill the priestly role of interceding with God, for others, through prayer (Ephesians 6:18). We pray to the Father (Matthew 6:6-9), through the Son (I Timothy 2:5), and under the guidance of the Holy Spirit (Romans 8:26-27). The Bible actually refers to us as a priesthood in I Peter 2:5,9.

The Body of Christ is a term used to describe the interconnection and interdependence that believers have, and the way they use their respective spiritual gifts for the edification of God's church (I Corinthians 12:1-31).

I Peter 2:9 refers to the body of believers as a *holy nation*. We are citizens of this nation and our eternal home is in heaven (Philippians 3:20). Regardless of our earthly nationality, as believers we are aliens in whichever land we are now living (I Peter 2:11).

In order to honor some particularly worthy people, the Roman Catholic Church has made a practice of conferring sainthood upon them. However, the Bible refers to *all* believers as *saints* (Psalm 116:15; Daniel 7:18; Ephesians 1:15; Revelation 5:8; 19:8; Psalms 30:4; 31:23; 34:9).

The most prevalent designation for the elect of God is *Christian* (Acts 11:26). The term "born-again Christian" is redundant, because all Christians "must be born again" (John 3:6-7). Unless one has been born anew, or again, by the Spirit, one is *not* a Christian. The term non-born-again Christian would be an oxymoron.

Finally, Christ calls His true followers *the church* (Matthew 16:18). The apostle's creed states, "I believe in the holy catholic church." This refers to the church universal, not the Roman Catholic Church. The church is universal, because God has chosen its people—from the beginning of time, out of every tongue, tribe, nationality, and country on Earth (Revelation 7:9-10).

Anyone of the aforementioned names for God's people could be used in heaven. But one thing is assured, we won't be referring to the citizens there by any denominational names, such as Baptist, Methodist, Presbyterian, Lutheran, Assemblies of God, Nazarene, Quaker, Roman Catholic, Anglican, Othrodox, etc. These divisions have occurred purely on account of man-made differences, based on individual interpretations of Scripture. In heaven, we will have perfect unity, based on perfect knowledge. There will be no differences. Early on, the church displayed perfect harmony (Acts 2:42-47), but it wasn't long before disunity developed (Acts 6:1; 11:1-2; 15:1-2).

It was Jesus' prayer that all believers would be "brought into complete unity" (John 17:23). In Ephesians 4:23, Paul reiterates Christ's plea when he writes, "make every effort to keep the unity of the spirit in the bond of peace." He then goes on to illustrate, in verses 4-6, some very good reasons for a oneness. He says there is "one body," "one spirit," "called to one hope," "one Lord," "one faith," "one baptism," "one God and Father of all."

In I Corinthians 3:1-17, we read of Paul's attempts to squelch a division that was developing in the church of Corinth. People had been focusing on men, not God. This is still true today.

Throughout the two thousand years of church history, the body of believers has continued to divide, over and over again, until today there are more than three hundred Christian denominations.

Not every person in each of these denominations is a believer, but the Lord knows those who are His (II Timothy 2:19). One day He will literally "weed" out the counterfeits. Jesus said that every house of worship would have a mixture of "wheat" (believers) and "weeds" (pretenders) (Matthew 13:24-30). Only the wheat will be gathered to heaven where we will all be of one mind, in perfect unity, and having perfect knowledge of our triune God (I Corinthians 13:12).

In summary, heaven will be filled with an entire community of Christian neighbors, whose company we will enjoy forever. Hebrews 12: 22-24 explains it like this: "You have come to Mount Zion, to the heavenly Jerusalem, the city of the living God. You have come to thousands upon thousands of angels in joyful assembly, to the church of the first born, whose names are written in heaven. You have come to God, the judge of all men, to the spirits of righteous men made perfect, to Jesus the mediator of a new covenant...."

That is something toward which we can all look with great anticipation and say with that Old Testament saint, Job, "How my heart yearns within me" (Job 19:27).

Chapter
SIX

The Presence of God

*O*ne of the great pleasures of being ushered into the third heaven will be the privilege of seeing God face to face. This is the God in whom we have believed, but whom we have never seen. We believe that He exists, purely on faith, and trust in the verity of the Bible.

Hebrews11: 6 warns us that "...without faith it is impossible to please God, because anyone who comes to Him must believe that He exists and that He rewards those who earnestly seek Him."

The faith that pleases God is defined in Hebrews 11:1 as "...being sure of what we hope for and certain of what we do not see." Furthermore, even this faith is not innate, it is a gift from God (Ephesians 2:8).

How can we believers be so certain that God exists? There are three reasons why I personally believe that God is truly a living being.

First, because He changed my life. That is definitely something I could never have done on my own. When I was spiritually dead in my sins, with no inclination toward pleasing

45

God (Genesis 6:5), He made me alive (Ephesians 2:4). He changed my whole perspective on life, restructured my entire worldview, and He gave me a fresh start. II Corinthians 5:17 says that "…if anyone is in Christ, he is a new creation, the old has gone, the new has come." God did that for me, and even if I had no further proof of His existence, that would suffice.

The second reason for my strong faith in the reality of God is His Word, the Bible. This is God's special revelation to His children (Deuteronomy 29:29; II Timothy 3:16-17). It is called "special" because it has a specific message to a specific group of people—believers. Unbelievers cannot understand the Bible (I Corinthians 2:13-14).

This is a book that guides my life and gives me wisdom. Though I have failed many times to put its precepts into practice, I've repeatedly tested them and found them to be absolutely and utterly infallible.

The Bible has, throughout the centuries, had many critics, but it has outlived them all. Time after time archeological explorations have uncovered civilizations previously unknown except in the pages of God's Holy Word (e.g., the Hittites).

The third reason for my certainty in God's existence is found in creation. This is known as general or natural revelation. Its message is to a "general" audience about general and natural evidence for God's existence. While God's Word is not available to, nor understood by, everyone, the beautiful creation is readily evident (thus the term "general revelation"). Eighteenth century theologian, philosopher, and apologist Jonathan Edwards, in his classic treatise entitled *Works*, has said, "There is nothing more certain than, that the universe somewhere contains an infinite uncaused being." Edwards was explaining that God is the ultimate, or first, cause of all that exists.

In Nature, we find a perfect order, design, and complexity that did not just happen. It cannot be, as Francis Schaeffer so aptly put it, "the result of time plus matter plus chance" (*He Is There and He Is Not Silent*).

Romans 1:19-20 offers a very succinct statement on "general revelation." It reads: "...what may be known about God is plain to them, because God has made it plain to them. For since the creation of the world God's invisible qualities...have been clearly seen, being understood from what has been made, so that men are without excuse."

Before becoming a Christian, I was an avid evolutionist. However, within six months of my conversion, God revealed to me the irrationality and improbability of the evolutionary position on origins.

Recently, *USA Today* reported on the unraveling of the mystery of the human genetic code—the genome. This code was found to contain some 3.5 billion letters within the countless DNA molecules. These molecules, in turn, make up the numerous genes that comprise the forty-six human chromosomes (twenty-two pairs of autosomes and two sex chromosomes).

DNA is a double stranded chain of nucleic acids that are twisted upon themselves. If all of the DNA chains in one human body could be unwound and laid end to end, they would reach from Washington, D.C., to Anchorage, Alaska.

If just one of the 3.5 billion letters is missing, or even out of sequence, the result will be death, or at least the development of a serious congenital defect.

Let's now look at the odds of a smaller number of genetic letters being aligned in a predetermined sequence, merely by chance.

First we'll begin with the chance that three letters, A, B, and C, will line up in just that order, by chance. To do that, we'll take three toy blocks, each having one of those letters printed on all six sides, and throw them out on the floor. To measure the odds of three things aligning properly (in this case the letters A-B-C, rather than B-A-C, C-B-A, etc.), we simply multiply 1x2x3=6. Thus the odds are one out of six. By adding a fourth block, the letter D, the odds become 1x2x3x4=24, or one out of twenty four. Add the fifth, E, and the odds rise to one out of one hundred twenty. With the sixth, the letter F, the odds climb to one out of seven hundred twenty.

By the time we reach the number 200, the odds of proper alignment are a staggering one out of ten to the three hundred sixty fourth power. For you non-mathematicians, a power is determined by the number of zeros in the number; thus ten is ten to the first power, one hundred is ten to the second power, one thousand is ten to the third power, one million is ten to the sixth power, etc. Thus the odds of two hundred letters becoming properly aligned, purely by chance, are one out of one with three hundred sixty four zeros following it.

The reason for using the number two hundred is that this is the number of letters found in one molecule of DNA. However, the least number required for that first cell to have developed by chance, in that theoretical sea of primordial "soup," that evolutionists have put their faith in, would have been considerably greater.

Thus, while I don't need to see God to believe in Him, I'm certainly looking forward to it. I can echo the statement made by Job, "I myself will see Him with my own eyes…how my heart yearns within me" (Job 19:27).

The only person who has ever seen God and walked the earth to tell about it was Jesus Christ (John 1:18).

The only other person who even came close to seeing God was Moses. However, God told Moses, "You cannot see my face, for no one may see me and live" (Exodus 33:23).

Even though we can't "see" God, He is still very near to us. Paul says in Acts 17:27, while addressing a group of Athenian philosophers, that God is "…not far from each one of us."

God is omnipresent, ubiquitous. In Jeremiah 23:24, He tells us that He fills heaven and earth. In Psalm 139:7-10, we read, "Where can I go from your Spirit? Where can I flee from your presence? If I go up to the heavens, you are there; if I make my bed in the depths, you are there. If I rise on the wings of the dawn, if I settle on the far side of the sea, even there your hand will guide me, your right hand will hold me fast."

C.S. Lewis, commenting on the ubiquitous nature of God said, "We may ignore, but we can nowhere evade, the presence of God. The world is crowded with Him. He walks everywhere, incognito" (*Letters to Malcolm: Chiefly on Prayer*).

In heaven, we will see God's face—whatever that means (Revelation 21:4). In Matthew 5:8, Jesus tells us that the pure in heart will see God. The believers heart will be "pure" because God will make it so, when we have become glorified (Philippians 3:21). That is all very hard to comprehend in our present state of mind because we are also told that God is a Spirit (John 4:24). Of course, what we have here is a mystery, a "secret thing" (Deuteronomy 29:29), that will one day be revealed to us. That, too, is a matter of faith.

We have many examples within the pages of Scripture of the so-called anthropomorphic (man-like) statements regarding God, In II Chronicles 16:9 we read of His "eyes"; in I Peter 3:12, "ears"; Psalm 110:1, "hand"; I Peter 3:12, "face"; and Psalm 18:15, "nostrils."

God is not a man (Numbers 23:19), He is a spirit and so we should not expect to see these body parts on our God in heaven. But in whatever form we "see" Him, we will no doubt rejoice at the sight and fall down before Him in utter awe, reverence, and thanksgiving.

Revelation 21:3 reads, "Now the dwelling of God is with men, and He will live with them. They will be His people and He Himself will be their God."

Do you remember what your life was like before you became aware of God's presence? At that time, though God was near, you and I were numb to His existence. Now as you look back, it is hard to imagine how we could have ever faced life's challenges without Him. Well, as much as we are now aware of His influence in our lives, so much more will we be aware of this when we are living with Him, in His very presence, for all eternity.

In II Corinthians 5:14, Paul assures us, emphatically, that we will one day be in the presence of God.

In Jude 24, we read, "To Him who is able to keep you from falling and to present you before His glorious presence without fault and with great joy." Ephesians 5:27 also instructs us that Jesus will present us to the Father. Picture that. We are "presented" to God the Father by God the Son. The closing line of the popular hymn "Jesus Led Me All the Way" goes like this; "I will tell the saints and angels as I lay my burdens down, 'Jesus led me all the way.'" If Jesus is leading and guiding you in this present life, He will continue to do so upon your physical demise, and He will lead you directly to His Father's throne.

When Stephen, the first martyr under the new covenant, was dying, he saw Jesus "standing at the right hand of God" (Acts 7:56). Other Scriptures speak only of Jesus "sitting" at God's right hand (Psalm 110:1; Hebrews 1:3; Mark 16:19). Could it be that Jesus stood up to welcome His servant Stephen into heaven and to present him to God the Father? I think that is a reasonable assumption.

In Psalm 110:1, the words LORD and Lord have specific significance. We discussed this in Chapter Four, but its importance deserves further mention. When all large case letters are used, as in LORD, the Hebrew word *Yahweh* is meant. This was a name held in such high esteem that Jews would not even utter it; they only wrote it. *Yahweh* means "I Am" (Exodus 3:14). This is God the Father, the first person of the Godhead.

Lord, in the Hebrew, is *Adonai*. This refers to the second person of the trinity, the Son, the one who became the Incarnate One, Jesus the Christ.

Thus Psalm 110:1 would read, "The Father said to the Son, sit at my right hand" (author paraphrase).

Jesus, in the person of *Adonai*, has been with the Father since time began. He is now praying—and has always prayed for and interceded with the Father—for His sheep, the believers. In

Job 16:19-21 we read of His preincarnate role as intercessor: "Even now my witness is in heaven; my advocate is on high. My intercessor is my friend as my eyes pour out tears to God; on behalf of a man he pleads with God as a man pleads for his friend."

In John 17:9, 20, Jesus states that His prayers are exclusively for believers. In Romans 8:38 we also read that Jesus is at the Father's right hand, interceding for us.

I John 2:1 says, "We have one who speaks to the Father in our defense, Jesus Christ the Righteous One."

He is our advocate, our defense attorney. The vivid picture here is one of a courtroom, with Jesus standing before the "bar of God" pleading our case. The scene is completed by the presence of the prosecutor—the accuser (Revelation 12:10), Satan—arguing against us.

This picture is foretold in Zechariah 3:1-4, where we see the same courtroom, with four persons present: Joshua (the high priest); the angel of the Lord (Jesus); Satan: and God the Father. The text reads, "Then he showed me Joshua the high priest standing before the angel of the Lord, and Satan standing at his right side to accuse him. The Lord said to Satan, 'The Lord rebuke you, Satan! The Lord, who has chosen Jerusalem, rebuke you! Is not this man a burning stick snatched from the fire?' The angel said to those who were standing before him, 'Take off his filthy clothes.' Then He said to Joshua, 'See, I have taken away your sin, and I will put rich garments on you.'"

Satan accuses Joshua of being a sinner and unworthy of a place in heaven, and God defends him by saying that He has saved Joshua from the fires of Hell and made him holy. The rich garments mentioned in Zechariah 3:4 are Christ's imputed righteousness (see also II Corinthians 5:21; Isaiah 61:10).

If you have trusted Christ as your only means of salvation, having received Him by faith as your Lord and Savior, you can personalize this scene by putting your name in the place of Joshua.

Satan stands before God to accuse you of some sin. Jesus says to Satan, "I died to take away this person's sin. It has been forgiven and forgotten. I have saved (Bill, Sue, Tom, Chuck...) from the fires of hell and I have made this person holy in my Father's sight."

This fact is verified in Colossians 1:21-22 where we read, " Once you were alienated from God and were enemies in your minds because of your evil behavior. But now he has reconciled you by Christ's physical body through death to present you holy in His sight, without blemish and free from accusation."

The skeptic would say, "Show me God and I'll believe." On the other hand, the Christian says, "I believe; show me." Or, as it says in Mark 9:24, "I believe, help my unbelief."

One day, God will show Himself to us and we will live in His holy presence forever; because we did believe. Jesus said, "...blessed are those who have not seen and yet have believed" (John 20:29).

The Hebrew word for presence is *paneh*, literally meaning "face." David, in his longing to be with God uttered these words in prayer, " My heart says of you, ' Seek His face!' Your face, LORD, I will seek." If your heart is speaking to you in this same way, it is the Holy Spirit saying it. I would urge you to answer His plea by putting your faith in Jesus, and one day you will stand, with David, and all of the other believers, *corem Deo*—before the face of God.

SEVEN

Eternal Light

*I*n the third heaven, we will enjoy perpetual light—no darkness, no night. Revelation 22:5 reads, "There will be no more night. They will not need the light of a lamp or the light of the sun, for the Lord God will give them light...."

God is the source of all light and, for that matter, all other forms of energy. When He was creating the universe, God said, "Let there be light" (Genesis 1:3), and there was light. He spoke it into existence. God is, therefore, the ultimate cause of all light.

Light was formed during the first day of creation and God turned it off and on ("and the evening and the morning") until day four when He placed the Sun in the second heaven to provide Earth with light and energy for as long as the Earth would remain.

The Sun will have no purpose in the third heaven. In addition to giving light and energy to Earth, it currently participates in time divisions: day and night, as the earth spins on it's axis; years, as the earth orbits the Sun; and seasons, that relate to Earth's tilt and its varying distance from the

Sun during its eliptical orbit. Yes, the Sun now serves us well in these matters of time, but recall, from Chapter Four, that in heaven time will be no more. No reference points will be needed, for all perspective there will be eternal.

As stated above, the only source of light that we will need in the third heaven is God Himself. Revelation 21:23 tells us that "the glory of God gives it light."

This "glory" is what caused Moses' face to glow when he descended from Mt Sinai—and he hadn't even seen God face to face (Exodus 34:29-35).

In the prophet Isaiah's account of his vision of heaven (Isaiah 6:1-2), during which he saw the Lord Jesus seated on His throne, several lessons are to be learned.

First, he didn't see *Yahweh*, for the text uses the word Lord, and not LORD. The One he saw was *Adonai*—Jesus.

Next, this vision is compatible with, and not a contradiction of, the statement in Exodus 33:20 that no man would ever see *Yahweh* and live.

Lastly, from his view of the seraphs (a type of angelic being), we learn of the utter brightness of God's glory. The text describes these creatures as follows: "...each with six wings. With two they covered their faces, with two they covered their feet, and with two they were flying."

Two of their wings were for the sole purpose of shielding their eyes from the brilliant, blinding light that proceeds from the throne of God. These creatures have been before the face of God ever since their creation, and they will continue to be there for all eternity. Thus periodically, they need to protect their eyes from the blinding light of God's glory.

In Psalm 4:6, David entreats God to "let the light of your face shine upon us." David is now enjoying that light, the light of God's glory, as he resides in the third heaven with all of the faithful of ages past.

I John 1:5 tells us that "God is light: in Him there is no darkness." That word "light" applies in both a physical and spiritual sense.

Thus far, we have been speaking only of physical (visible) light. This is that small band of energy on the electromagnetic spectrum that resides between the infrared and the ultraviolet bands.

There is, however, another kind of light, about which the Scriptures have much to say. This light will also be part of the eternal light that we will enjoy in the third heaven; this is spiritual light.

As believers, we have all had varying degrees of experience with spiritual light, but, compared to that which we will encounter in heaven, it is but a flicker, a minute radiance—like comparing the glow of a lightening bug on a summer's night to the noonday sun.

II Corinthians 4:6 describes our initial experience with this light: "For God, who said, 'Let light shine out of darkness,' made His light shine in our hearts to give us the light of the knowledge of the glory of God in the face of Christ." Psalm 18: 28 reads, "My God turns my darkness into light." This refers to spiritual "darkness" and spiritual "light."

When Jesus said, "I am the Light of the world" (John 8:12), it was this spiritual light to which He referred. In John 3:19, Jesus said that "...Light has come into the world, but men loved darkness instead of light...." In II Samuel 22:29, David says, "You are my lamp, O LORD; the LORD turns my darkness into light."

Jonathan Edwards, whom the World Book Encyclopedia portrays as "the outstanding theologian and scholar of colonial New England in the 1700s," wrote, "There is such a thing as a Spiritual and Divine Light, immediately imparted to the soul by God, of a different nature from any that is obtained by natural means" (*The Rational Biblical Theology of Jonathan Edwards, Volume I*).

This "imparting" of spiritual light occurs "immediately," at the moment of our new-birth, so that the believer can "see the Kingdom of God" (John 3:3).

Songwriter John Newton alluded to this experience in his classic hymn "Amazing Grace": "I once was blind but now I see." His blindness had not been physical but spiritual.

The "seeing" mentioned by Jesus and Newton is literally comprehension. We use this distinction when we ask the question, "Do you 'see' what I mean?" We are saying, "Do you understand or comprehend what I am telling you?"

The Holy Spirit, who thus enables us to see the reflected light of the gospel, emanating from the pages of God's Holy Word, imparts the "light" of understanding. Without this spiritual illumination we would not be able to understand the Bible, or any other spiritual truth. I Corinthians 2:14 explains that, "The man without the Spirit does not accept the things that come from the Spirit of God, for they are foolishness to him, and he cannot understand them, because they are spiritually discerned." Note, the text says, "he cannot," not, "he will not"; this is not a matter of will, but capacity. All Scripture comes from the Spirit of God (II Timothy 3:16) and the Spirit of God must be residing within us to "guide" us "into all truth" (John16:13).

Edwards, in total agreement says, "He that is spiritually enlightened truly appreciates and sees it" (*The Rational Biblical Theology of Jonathan Edwards, Volume I*). The "it" he refers to is the truth of God's Word.

The divine light that emanates from the pages of Scripture illumines our souls and gives us direction in life. I John 1:7 reads, "...if we walk in the light, as He is in the light, we have fellowship with one another...." Walking in the Light means following the precepts, the commands, the absolute truths that are very clearly revealed in Scripture. In other words, it means living according to the Word of God.

David says, in Psalm 119:105, "Your Word is a lamp to my feet and a light for my path," and in verse 130, "The unfolding of your words gives light; it gives understanding to the simple."

The apostle Peter tells us that the "word" is like "a light shining in a dark place" (II Peter 1:19). This "dark place" is the soul prior to the illumination that is accomplished by the Holy Spirit. It was a sin-darkened soul that was blind to spiritual truth.

Any person that has received Christ, "the Light of the World" (John 8:12), has been enlightened, so that though "you were once darkness...now you are light in the Lord" (Ephesians 5:8).

The spiritual light that we have now will pale in comparison to the light that we will ultimately have when we reside in the third heaven. This will be discussed in greater detail in Chapter Sixteen.

Suffice it to say, our earthly minds do not have the capacity to comprehend, understand, or assimilate all that we will one day know.

As Jesus was about to close His thirty-three years of earthly life, He said this to His disciples: "I have much more to say to you, more than you can now bear" (John 16:12). One day, He will share all of those things with them, and us, for then we will have the spiritual and intellectual capacity to comprehend those great truths. In other words, we will be able to "bear" His words.

EIGHT

The Tree of Life

*T*he apostle John, writing in Revelation 22:1-2, explains that in his vision of the third heaven he saw a "river of the water of life, as clear as crystal, flowing from the throne of God and of the Lamb, down the middle of the great street of the city. On each side of the river stood the tree of life…and its leaves are for the healing of the nations."

This is the same life-giving tree which had been among the many trees that God had planted in the Garden of Eden. Genesis 2:9 reads, "In the middle of the garden were the tree of life and the tree of the knowledge of good and evil."

The tree of life was to have provided eternal, life-giving sustenance to Adam and Eve, for as long as they chose to obey God. This should have been easy, since God had placed merely one restriction on their otherwise free reign upon the earth. God had imposed only one commandment, one test of their willingness to obey Him. He said, "You are free to eat from any tree in the garden; but you must not eat from the tree of the knowledge of good and evil, for when you eat of it you will surely die" (Genesis 2:16-17).

Of course, as we well know, Adam and Eve both failed the test. They broke the only law that God had required of them; they sinned. Thus, the "fall" of mankind.

Romans 5:12 summarizes the devastating effects of this disobedience when it says, "Therefore, just as sin entered the world through one man, and death through sin, ...in this way death came to all men, because all sinned."

The spiritual death of Adam and Eve came immediately; their physical death was graciously delayed by God for nearly nine hundred years (Genesis 5:5).

Adam had been created in the image of God, as a perfect specimen of humanity. He was of sound body, soul, and spirit. When he fell, his fall affected four specific relationships. It was in essence a four-fold fall.

Fall One

Adam and God had been friends. They had walked together in the garden in perfect agreement. However, that relationship immediately changed when they disagreed over God's one and only commandment. Thus, their fellowship was broken. Amos 3:3 poses the question, "Can two walk together unless they have agreed...?"

Genesis 3:8 relates the unfortunate account, that Adam and Eve "heard the sound of the Lord God as He was walking in the garden...and they hid from the Lord God among the trees." Adam, when discovered, told God, "...I was afraid...so I hid."

Thus, Adam had fallen spiritually; he was immediately rendered spiritually dead. He now had a *spiritual* problem.

Fall Two

After Adam and Eve had eaten the forbidden fruit, " The eyes of both of them were opened, and they realized they were naked, so they sewed fig leaves together and made coverings for themselves" (Genesis 3:7). Their self-esteem had now been lowered. They were ashamed of their natural nakedness, and, as a result of the fall, we've all been ashamed ever since. They had fallen from themselves. Their egos were wounded, and they now had a *psychological* problem.

Fall Three

After they had sinned, Adam and Eve began to have marital problems. Eve had defiled her husband's caveat concerning the forbidden fruit and ate some of it (Genesis 3:6). This was done in spite of the fact that her husband had told her of God's warning and prohibition concerning the tree of the knowledge of good and evil—a warning that God had given Adam even before Eve had been created.

Furthermore, Adam had stood by and watched Eve break the rule of God. This was in direct opposition to God's instruction that a man is to be the spiritual head of his family (I Corinthians 11:3). Of course, at the time of the fall, Adam's "family" consisted of only the two of them.

Sadly, when God asked Adam why he had eaten the fruit, he answered, " The woman you put here with me, she gave me some fruit from the tree, and I ate it" (Genesis 3:12). Adam had tried to pass the buck—first to God, then to Eve.

This resulted in the first marital spat—the first breach of a perfect union that would ultimately lead to the current divorce rate of one in two marriages. They had fallen from each other, and they now had a *sociological* problem.

Fall Four

Finally, Adam and Eve fell from the environment. It had been very "user friendly," but now it became hostile. In Genesis 3:17-19, God informed Adam that, "Because you listened to your wife and ate from the tree about which I commanded you, 'You must not eat of it,' cursed is the ground because of you; through painful toil you will eat of it all the days of your life. It will produce thorns and thistles for you, and you will eat the plants of the field. By the sweat of your brow you will eat your food until you return to the ground...." Our first parents now had an *ecological* problem.

The final act of earthly punishment for Adam and Eve was eviction from their home in the Garden of Eden. Genesis 3:23-24 tells of their banishment: "And the LORD God said, 'The man has now become like one of us, knowing good and evil. He must not be allowed to reach out his hand and take also from the tree of life, and eat and live forever.' So the LORD God banished him from the Garden of Eden to work the ground from which he had been taken. After he drove the man out, he placed on the East Side of the Garden of Eden cherubim and a flaming sword flashing back and forth to guard the way to the tree of life."

Thus, they had lost paradise. This would be the last contact that any living human being would ever have with the tree of life this side of the third heaven, the new paradise.

In Revelation 2:7, John tells us that Jesus assures believers, "To him that overcomes, I will give the right to eat from the tree of life which is in the Paradise of God."

If you have received Jesus, by faith, as your Savior and Lord, you have already overcome, and one day, in the third heaven, you will eat from that same tree.

A friend of mine once came to me for some spiritual advice. It seems that his pastor had repeatedly told him, and others, that they needed to be "feeding daily from the tree of life." My friend wanted to know how he could do that. The answer of course is that *no one can do that until they have passed from here into the third heaven*. After all, that's where the tree of life is.

While his pastor may have been well intentioned, he was terribly misinformed. We are told to feed, not on the tree of life, but on God's Word. We are encouraged to do this by Peter (I Peter 2:2), by Paul (I Corinthians 3:2), by the author of Hebrews (Hebrews 5:12-14), by Moses (Deuteronomy 8:3), and by God (Ezekial 3:1-3).

Jesus told Peter to feed His flocks—His sheep, His lambs—those for whom He had died (John 21:15,17). The implication was to feed them spiritual truths. Peter did just that by becoming a first century evangelist, the author of two epistles, and, probably, the Gospel of Mark.

When Jesus died, He was nailed to a "tree." "He Himself bore our sins in his body on the tree" (I Peter 2:24). For Jesus, it was a tree of death. He did this "so that we might die to sins and live for righteousness" (I Peter 2:24). His "tree of death" has given us ultimate access to the "tree of life."

If you have put your faith in Christ and His death on behalf of your sin—which was His purpose for dying on that "tree," the cross of Calvary—then you too can join other believers in the third heaven and eat from the tree of life in the paradise of God.

That tree will then do for us what God had originally intended for it to do for Adam and Eve: it will sustain us eternally.

Jesus said, "I am the resurrection and the life. He who believes in me will live, even though he dies; and whoever lives and believes in me will never die" (John 11:25-26). We'll never die because we will finally be permitted to "take also from the tree of life and eat, and live forever" (Genesis 3:22).

Part C

"What Will We Be Like?"

"There is no need to be worried by facetious people who try to make the Christian hope of 'Heaven' ridiculous by saying they do not want 'to spend eternity playing harps.' The answer to such people is that if they cannot understand books written for grown-ups, they should not talk about them. All the scriptural imagery (harps, crowns, gold, etc.) is, of course, a merely symbolic attempt to express the inexpressible. People who take these symbols literally might as well think that when Christ told us to be like doves, He meant that we were to lay eggs."

— C.S.Lewis
Mere Christianity

Chapter NINE

Just Like Jesus

hen we finally reach the third heaven, we will have attained a state of being, exceeded only by God Himself. Apart from certain divine attributes that will always remain the exclusive domain of the Trinity, we will be like Jesus.

I John 3:2 serves as a reminder to all believers that "now we are children of God, and what we will be has not yet been made known. But we know that when He appears, we shall be like Him, for we shall see Him as He is."

The apostle Paul presents the same idea in Philippians 3:20-21, where he has written, "Our citizenship is in heaven. And we eagerly await a Savior from there, the Lord Jesus Christ, who, by the power that enables Him to bring everything under His control, will transform our lowly bodies so that they will be like His glorious body."

In heaven, where He now sits at God the Father's right hand (Mark 19:19; Romans 8:34), Jesus has a body—a glorified body. What that means exactly, remains one of the mysteries of God. That is why John said in I John 3:2 that "what we will be has not been made known."

Before the incarnation—a time when "the Word became flesh" (John 1:14) and Jesus became a man—He had been, like the Father and the Holy Spirit, a spirit Himself. When He became a man, His spirit took up residence in a human body.

In Hebrews 10:5, Jesus makes this rather profound and informative statement, in addressing His Father, "a body you prepared for me." That "body" was in the form of a tiny embryo, and it was placed in the womb of the virgin Mary by the Holy Spirit. The spirit of Christ then entered that embryonic human frame and was ultimately born as the baby Jesus. God had done a "new thing" (Jeremiah 31:32), something that had never been done before or since.

An angel had told Mary, "The Holy Spirit will come upon you…. So the holy one to be born will be called the Son of God" (Luke 1:35). Thus Mary was merely the chosen instrument which God used to send His Son into the world of man, as a man—while at the same time retaining His divine nature. Jesus never bore any genetic relationship to Mary and was thus sinless.

Philippians 2:6-7 explains that Jesus, "being in very nature God," that is, He was a spirit, took on the "very nature" of a man and was "made in human likeness."

This body, the totally human body that Christ possessed for His thirty-three years on earth was exactly like ours—with the crucial exception of the presence of sin.

In that body, Jesus could be present in but one place at a time. In it, He experienced pain, fatigue, and thirst. His body was, for most of His life, limited by the very laws of nature that He Himself had created. At times however, being God, He was able to suspend those laws and thus walk on water, create food, and transform His earthly body, temporarily, into a glorified one (Mark 9:2-4).

When Jesus died, He died a physical death. But, instead of allowing His body to undergo a natural decay (Psalm 16:10), the Father raised Him with a newly formed, glorified body—the one He would occupy for all eternity.

It was that glorified body that His disciples viewed after the resurrection. But, for some unexplained reason, there seemed always to be a delay in their recognition of Him.

The men on the Emmaus road were "kept from recognizing Him" at first (Luke 24:16). Later, however, "their eyes were opened and they recognized Him" (Luke 24:31).

At the tomb, on resurrection morning, Mary "saw Jesus standing there, but did not recognize that it was Jesus" (John 20:14). They exchanged several words before He spoke her name and then, suddenly, she knew who He was (John 20:16).

Later that evening, "when the disciples were together, with the doors locked for fear of the Jews, Jesus came and stood among them and said, 'Peace be with you.' After He said this, He showed them His hands and His side" (John 20:19-20).

He had to show them His nail pierced wrists and the spear torn side before they knew that He was the Lord.

Note that Jesus had entered a locked room, without the benefit of a door. This is a further indication of the capacity of a glorified body to suspend natural laws. This glorified state on earth lasted forty days (Acts 1:3), during which Jesus spent a great deal of time teaching His disciples. Then one day, suddenly, He "was taken up before their very eyes, and a cloud hid Him from their sight" (Acts 1:9).

From other verses in Scripture, we know that He returned to His Father (John 16:28: Psalm 110:1: Hebrews 1:3: Mark 16:19), but He went back to the third heaven, not as a spirit, the way He had been before His incarnation, but with a visible glorified body.

John would see Jesus again before he died (Revelation 1:12-13), and we too will see Him in heaven, because we will be like Him.

Our glorification will be the consummation of a gradual process of perfection, righteousness, and holiness that God has been working in us since the day that we were born again (Philippians 1:6; 2:13).

Romans 8:29-30 summarizes this process: "For those God foreknew He also predestined to be conformed to the likeness of His Son.... And those He predestined, He also called; those He called He also justified; those He justified, He also glorified."

Predestined. Called. Justified. Glorified. This is a chain reaction that begins and ends in eternity. Each link in the chain is dependent upon the one preceding it. Thus, God predestines our salvation in eternity past (Ephesians 1:4), then at some time during our earthly life He calls us inwardly, through the working of the Holy Spirit in our hearts. This latter step in the chain reaction is called being "born again." We are regenerated from a state of spiritual deadness to a state of being spiritually alive (Ephesians 2:4; Colossians 2:13). As a result, we are able to recognize our sinful state, repent, and ask for God's forgiveness (I John 1:9). This is done purely by faith, which is itself, a gift from God (Ephesians 2:8-9).

Once we have taken these steps, under the guidance and power of the Holy Spirit, we become justified. At this point, we have received the righteousness of Christ, by imputation, and He has taken our sin upon Himself (II Corinthians 5:21). We also appear to be perfectly holy in God's sight (Colossians 1:22).

The last step in the chain reaction is our glorification. This happens only after our physical death when our soul is united with this glorified body.

Because this is a chain reaction, once it begins it is, by definition, irreversible. Romans 11:29 assures us that God's "call" is "irrevocable." Thus, the one whom He has predestined, in eternity past, He will ultimately and assuredly glorify in the future.

One element in our Christian experience is missing in this "golden chain" reaction: sanctification. The reason for this omission is often misunderstood. Our predestination, calling, justification, and glorification are each solely the work of God; they are on God's part, divine operations, monergistic (one working).

Sanctification, on the other hand, is a result of cooperation and synergism (working together). We cooperate with the Holy Spirit as we avail ourselves to His teaching in Scripture (I Thessalonians 2:13) and appropriate and apply those teachings in our activities of daily living. Thus, Jesus prayed to the Father, "Sanctify them by the truth; your word is truth" (John 17: 17). Apart from the study of God's Word, we can never attain *any* degree of sanctification.

The process of progressive sanctification begins, inevitably and immediately, at the time of our new birth. As it continues, our behavior and world view change in accordance with the absolute truths that we have learned in Scripture (Psalm 119:9). This does not occur however, without the synergistic effect of the Holy Spirit working in and through us to produce the change.

We will never become absolutely perfect through this gradual process of sanctification, although some attain more spiritual maturity than others do. Ultimately however, we will all be on a level plane, as we experience our glorification in the third heaven and receive our spiritual bodies.

Paul explains this in detail in I Corinthians 15:35-44: "But someone may ask, 'How are the dead raised? With what kind of body will they come?' How foolish! What you sow does not come to life unless it dies. When you sow, you do not plant the body that will be, just a seed, perhaps of wheat or of something else. But God gives it a body as He has determined, and to each kind of seed He gives its own body. All flesh is not the same: Men have one kind of flesh, animals have another, birds another, and fish another. There are also heavenly bodies and there are earthly bodies; but the splendor of the heavenly bodies is one kind, and the splendor of the earthly bodies is another. The sun has one kind of splendor, the moon another, and the stars another; and star differs from star in splendor.

So it will be with the resurrection of the dead. The body that is sown is perishable, it is raised imperishable; it is sown in dishonor, it is raised in glory; it is sown in weakness, it is raised in power; it is sown a natural body, it is raised a spiritual body."

Thus far Paul has told us that our heavenly bodies will be, imperishable (they'll last forever), glorious, powerful, and spiritual.

Paul continues, "If there is a natural body, there is also a spiritual body. So it is written: 'The first man Adam, became a living being,' 'the last Adam, a life-giving spirit'" (I Corinthians 15:44-45). This reference to the "last Adam" is pointing to Jesus. Whereas, the first Adam gave physical life to all men through his genes, Jesus, the last Adam gives eternal life to His followers through His Spirit.

Paul then says, "The spiritual did not come first, but the natural, and after that the spiritual. The first man was of the dust of the earth, the second man from heaven. As was the earthly man, so also are those who are of the earth; and as is the man from heaven, so are those who are of heaven. And just as we have borne the likeness of the earthly man, so shall we bear the likeness of the man from heaven" (I Corinthians 15:46-49).

This is our greatest hope and that to which we should all look forward—our glorification.

There is much talk today about the overwhelming despair that is so prevalent among America's young people. I believe this despondency results from a lack of this eternal hope. We, as a society have removed all discussion of God and eternity from our institutions of learning. Today our kids are taught that they are cosmic accidents: that they have arisen out of the slime of some imagined primordial sea, and that when life is over, they pass into oblivion. Furthermore their lives seem to be unplanned and purposeless. It's no wonder that they're in a state of depression.

One verse in God's Word, if taught to them, could dispel these notions. II Corinthians 5:5 reads, "Now it is God who has made us for this very purpose and has given us the Spirit as a deposit, guaranteeing what is to come."

First it says, "God...has made us." We haven't evolved by chance, we were designed. Next, we're told that there was a purpose for our being born, a reason for our existence. Psalm 139:16 assures us, "All the days ordained for me were written in your book before one of them came to be." We just have to find that purpose, that plan of God, as He leads us to discover it. Finally, Paul says that God guarantees "what is to come." This guarantee is for those who have received Christ by faith and are indwelt by His Holy Spirit.

There is purpose in life. God has each of us here for a particular reason. The Westminster Shorter Catechism says, "Man's chief end is to glorify God and enjoy Him forever." Now that's a purpose if I ever heard one.

Paul also explains God's consummate purpose for His children: "Now we know that if the earthly tent we live in is destroyed, we have a building from God, an eternal house in heaven, not built by human hands. Meanwhile we groan, longing to be clothed with our heavenly dwelling" (II Corinthians 5:1-2). The "earthly tent" of which Paul speaks is our physical body. The "eternal house" is our glorified body. (We'll discuss these in greater detail in Chapter Sixteen as we discuss the concept of the soul.)

God's ultimate purpose for us is our perfection through glorification. This will please God immeasurably. This, I believe, is why the psalmist wrote in Psalm 116:15, "Precious in the sight of the Lord is the death of His saints." We'll be "precious in His sight" because we'll be just like Jesus.

Chapter TEN

No More Tears

*I*n Revelation chapters 21 and 22, the apostle John gives us a glimpse of the place where we will spend eternity. He assures us that God "...will wipe away every tear from their eyes. There will be no more death or mourning or crying or pain, for the old order of things has passed away" (Revelation 21:4).

The "old order" refers to the situation here on planet Earth and the condition that has resulted from living under a curse. As long as we are here the curse will affect each one of us. That curse includes death—a cause for mourning, pain, and crying.

In Genesis 3:16, because of the "fall," God said to Eve, "I will greatly increase your pains in child bearing; with pain you will give birth to children." Every mother that is now reading this book can certainly identify with that portion of the curse.

To Adam, in verse17, God promised a life of "painful toil." Think of the aches and pains that result from a long period of physical exertion.

Heaven, on the other hand, will be a place of unending joy. I once heard joy defined by Jeanie Ford (Leighton's wife and Billy Graham's sister) as "an attitude of the heart that has its roots in God." She and Leighton certainly had to call on that attitude when their son Sandy died while undergoing open heart surgery. In heaven, our heart's attitude will definitely be more deeply "rooted" in God than it is now, and, as a result, our joy will overflow in the worship of Him.

In the third heaven, we will never have reason to shed tears caused by the death of a loved one. Isaiah tells us that God "will swallow up death forever. The Sovereign Lord will wipe away tears from all faces" (Isaiah 25:8).

In Psalm 16:11, David speaks of his eternal salvation and the resulting "attitude of the heart," when he says to God, "You have made known to me the path of life; you have filled me with joy in your presence, with eternal pleasures at your right hand."

The "path of life" of which David spoke is Christ. Jesus said that He is "the Way, the Truth, and the Life" (John 14:6).

In heaven there will be no trouble to cause us sadness, regret, mourning, fear, disappointment, or despair.

Jesus warned that, "In this world you will have trouble" (John 16:33). It is inevitable in our world. But further on in the verse, He says that we should "be of good cheer," because He has "overcome the world." That means that one day he will rescue us from these earthly woes and take us to heaven, where further trouble will be nonexistent.

Psalm 34:6,17 also testify to the fact that the Lord will ultimately deliver us from trouble.

Jesus left the solitude, glory, and safety of heaven to assume the form of a man, enter a trouble filled world, live a perfect life, and then die on a cross for His followers; His sheep (John 10:15). The author of Hebrews writes that Jesus "...for the joy set before Him endured the cross, scorning its shame, and sat down at the right hand of God" (Hebrews 12:2).

Jesus looked past the pain and shame of Calvary's cross toward the joy of being on His eternal throne, at the right hand of His Father.

Isaiah predicts our state of perpetual joy when he says, "They will enter Zion with singing; everlasting joy will crown their heads. Gladness and joy will overtake them, and sorrow and sighing will flee away" (Isaiah 35:10). Given the choice, none of us, nor any of those currently residing in the third heaven, will ever want to return to this trouble filled earth again.

A recent *USA Today* article (August 2000), reported that the Eli Lilly Pharmaceutical Corporation sells 2.5 billion dollars worth of the anti-depressant Prozac annually. The average cost is ninety dollars per month, or one thousand eighty dollars per year. That means that approximately 2.5 million people take that anti-depressant alone, and there are many more kinds of anti-depressant drugs on the market.

For years, anti-anxiety agents—such as Valium, Librium, Serax, and Xanax, to name just a few—have led all pharmaceuticals in the race for dollars.

What this all adds up to is a great number of depressed and anxious people. It seems that the farther society gets from God and His Word, the greater the stress, anxiety, depression, and, especially of late, rage (e.g., "road rage").

Francis Schaeffer had it right when, writing in *A Chritian Manifesto*, he said that we are living in a "post-Christian society." America, he said, has "lost its Christian consensus." He said that the main goals that most Americans are trying to achieve are those of "personal peace and prosperity." How sad that in the early years of the twenty first century—a time when we are living during a great economic boom—personal peace has evaded most Americans.

Make no mistake: we Christians are not immune from either anxiety or depression. However, we do have something to look forward to that other humans don't. We have heaven with its eternal joy and freedom from emotional disorders.

Even now, while we are living on the earth, the Lord has given us a remedy—one that far too few of us utilize. In Philippians 4:6-7, we find a solution to emotional upheaval: "Do not be anxious about anything, but in everything, by prayer and petition, with thanksgiving, present your requests to God. And the peace of God, which transcends all understanding, will guard your hearts and your minds in Christ Jesus."

In our present state, we are prone to think of joy as synonymous with pleasure. But that brings joy down to the level of the physical (or sensual). We often speak of joy in terms of satisfying our five senses: the joy of eating, because it *tastes* so good; of enjoying beautiful music, because it *sounds* so good; of *smelling* a rose, because the aroma is so pleasing; of *seeing* a beautiful landscape, because it looks so good; of enjoying a back rub, because it *feels* so good.

The joy of heaven will not be like any of those things. We will not be focused on the physical but rather the spiritual. It will be spiritual fulfillment and attainment that will bring us real joy. The joy we now receive from spending some quality time alone with our spouse on a romantic second honeymoon will be superceded by the joy of being with Christ.

When Jesus was in Samaria, speaking with a woman near a well, his disciples asked Him if He wanted some lunch. Jesus answered, "I have food to eat that you know nothing about.... My food is to do the will of Him who sent me and to finish His work" (John 4:32,34). Doing the will of God, not satisfying His physical need for food, was foremost in Jesus' thoughts; that is what brought Him real joy. In heaven, we will have the perfect mind of Christ; we will be just like Him and be in utter agreement with His desires. That alone will be our greatest cause for joy.

In the third heaven, we will always be in God's perfect will. The Bible distinguishes (not in words, but in teaching) between God's "perfect" and "permissive" will. We are taught that, from time to time, God permits us to roam outside of His perfect will into the domain of His permissive will.

Within His perfect will there is always peace, rest, joy, contentment, order, and security. Outside, however, in His permissive will, we can experience anxiety, stress, restlessness, chaos, fear, and disappointment.

The best analogy that I've ever heard to distinguish these two aspects of God's will is that of a hurricane.

The "eye" of the hurricane represents God's perfect will. Therein, the sun is shining, the birds are singing, the air is still; it's a place of utter peace and solitude.

However, immediately outside of the eye, the utmost force of the storm is experienced. There is violence, chaos, frightening sights, pain, and death.

Our sovereign God has each of His children on a leash and He permits us to venture outside of His perfect will for several reasons.

First, in order that we might experience the contrast—just in case we've begun to take His grace for granted and have forgotten where we were, at one time in our life, without Him.

Then, He also wants us to realize that we are still totally dependent on Him—that without Him we will fall. He wants us to see that our weak will and basic sinful nature will lead us astray if we don't seek His face every day in prayer and through the study of His Word.

Finally, it is through adversity, in the midst of the "storms of life," that we grow spiritually as believers. The epistle of James reminds us of this: "Consider it pure joy, my brothers, whenever you face trials of many kinds, because you know that the testing of your faith develops perseverance. Perseverance must finish its work so that you may be mature and complete, not lacking anything" (James 1:2-4).

When we are in heaven, trials will be unnecessary to mature us because we will already have attained perfect spiritual development. This will occur at the very instant of our glorification. We'll finally be in the center of God's perfect will at all times. We'll experience perfect joy and never shed a single tear ever again.

Those of us in heaven will have absolutely no penchant for sin. We'll have no further lessons to learn. In our glorified state, we will have become all that God planned for us to be.

In his second epistle, Peter tells us about a nature— which we Christians now have in part—that will be fully consummated in heaven. It is a divine nature: "His divine power has given us everything we need for life and godliness through our knowledge of him who called us by His own glory and goodness. Through these He has given us His very great and precious promises, so that through them you may participate in the divine nature and escape the world caused by evil desires" (II Peter 1:3-4).

It is the shedding of tears, caused by pain or suffering, that God often uses to draw people to Jesus (John 6:44). C.S. Lewis said that pain and adversity are "God's megaphone, that He uses to get our attention" (*The Problem of Pain*).

In Jeremiah 50:4-6, the prophet speaks of this very issue: "In those days, at that time–the people of Israel and the people of Judah together will go in tears to seek the Lord their God. They will ask the way to Zion and will turn their faces toward it. They will come and bind themselves to the LORD in an everlasting covenant that will not be forgotten. My people have been lost sheep; their shepherds have led them astray and caused them to roam on the mountains. They wandered over mountain and hill and forgot their own resting place."

In those verses "Israel and Judah" refer to God's chosen, called by God from among both Jews and Gentiles.

"Zion" is heaven. "Lost sheep" are the elect before they receive Christ. The "shepherds" are preachers who do not believe the Word of God. "Their own resting place" which they forgot is God Himself. God used adversity and tears to stir their memories and draw them to Himself, their "resting place."

St. Augustine wrote, in a prayer to God, "Thou hast made us for thyself; and our hearts are restless until they find their rest in thee" (*The Confessions of St. Augustine, Part VII*).

Isaiah describes heaven—as the Holy Spirit has revealed it to him—as a place where "The sun will no more be your light by day, nor will the brightness of the moon shine on you, for the LORD will be your everlasting light, and your God will be your glory...and your days of sorrow will end" (Isaiah 60:19-20).

Jeremiah too encourages troubled believers when he writes that God says, "I will turn their mourning into gladness; I will give them comfort and joy instead of sorrow" (Jeremiah 31:13).

What a day that will be: when we can leave mourning, sorrow, sadness, and tears behind; when even the word "death" will be absent from our vocabulary; and when God will wipe those tears from our eyes and we can look forward to the experience of everlasting joy.

Chapter
ELEVEN

Past Things Forgotten

*A*re there some things in your past that you would
like to forget, but can't? If not, you are a very unique
person. Most of us have made some foolish decisions that
we'd like to be able to reverse. Certainly, we've all said
things that we wish we hadn't. We all have bad memories
that we'd like to have erased from our consciousness. Well,
I've got good news for each one of us: In heaven, those
things that have plagued our memories of the past will all
be forgotten.

In the sixty-fifth chapter of Isaiah, the prophet tells
about the third heaven and what it will be like. In verse 17
he quotes God as saying, "Behold, I will create new heavens
and a new earth. *The former things will not be remembered, nor will they come to mind*" (emphasis added). We
know that God is speaking of heaven in that verse of
Scripture, because He makes the same statement regarding
the "new heaven and new earth" in the opening verse of
Revelation chapter 21, which begins His final dissertation
on the third heaven.

It only stands to reason that heaven wouldn't be paradise if we carried all of the baggage from our previous life through its jeweled portals and onto its streets of gold.

If even one of our friends or family members is missing from the multitudes that will be gathered at the throne of God, we could not possibly experience eternal peace and rest knowing that they are elsewhere—in hell.

Proverbs 10:7 reads, "The memory of the righteous will be a blessing." Can we be blessed by remembering the eternal damnation of a loved one who never received Christ by faith? No, only "the memory of the righteous" will be retained within our souls, and they'll all be with us. In contrast however, the proverb goes on to relate that "the name of the wicked will rot." That is to say, his or her name will disappear from our memories.

In Matthew 7:21-23, Jesus tells about those unbelieving souls and their eternal destiny. "Not everyone who says to me, 'Lord, Lord,' will enter the kingdom of heaven, but only he who does the will of my Father who is in heaven. Many will say to me on that day, 'Lord, Lord, did we not prophesy in your name and in your name drive out demons and perform many miracles? Then I will tell them plainly, 'I never knew you. Away from me you evil doers!'"

Jesus said, "I never knew you" to those who were destined for hell. And for us, since we too will be like Jesus, it will be as though we "never knew" them.

One day at the close of office hours, my secretary informed me that Mary (not her real name). wanted to see me for a moment. I had an idea what Mary wanted and asked that she be sent back to my office immediately. Mary's estranged husband Tom (not his real name). had passed away one week before and I thought that she might want to talk about his death. I was right.

"Doctor," she said, "Do you think that Tom may have made an 'eleventh hour' decision before he died? You were with him, and he knew where you stood in regard to Jesus and the salvation of the soul. So could it be that he finally saw the light before he died without Christ in his heart?"

It is true that I had spoken with Tom about his life of alcoholism and his mocking attitude concerning Mary's profound faith in Christ, but my words had always fallen on deaf ears. Tom apparently never had the "ears to hear."

On the day in question, Tom was dying as a result of his alcohol addiction. His liver had failed and he was bleeding massively from ruptured veins in his esophagus. I did stay with him, as his lifeblood drained from his body, and we attempted to replace it as fast as we could. However, after over thirty units of blood given over a period of five hours, Tom went into shock and died.

Now, Mary sat there in my office, wondering if the man she had loved would be in heaven when she got there. I could only hope with her that he had seen the light and that God's grace had been extended to him at the last hour, as it had been extended to that thief on the cross (Luke 23:43).

"Mary," I said,"I'm not certain about Tom's last thoughts. I'm not sure whether they were on our Lord or not. But I am convinced of this. When you get to heaven, if Tom is there, you will rejoice. On the other hand, if he isn't there, it won't matter. As God told Isaiah, in chapter 65 verse 17, Tom won't be remembered, nor will he 'come to mind.'"

In Psalm 112:6, we read that "...a righteous man will be remembered forever." This means that all those we love, those that have been made righteous by the imputed righteousness of Christ (II Corinthians 5:21) will be remembered forever—because they'll be with us forever. However, the ones who have never received the gift of salvation and the resultant righteousness of Christ will be forgotten. Psalm 34:16 reads, "The face of the Lord is against those who do evil, to cut off the memory of them from the earth." If the memory of them is gone from the earth, then it will surely be gone from heaven as well.

81

I once heard a woman make this foolish statement, after losing her husband to death, "If John isn't in heaven, then I don't want to be there either." Why is that foolish? Because she is putting John before God. God will be there: God the Father, God the Son, and God the Holy Spirit. God's first commandment in the Decalog is, "You shall have no other gods before Me" (Exodus 20:3). This woman had put a "god" named John before the infinite, personal, sovereign Lord of the universe.

What that woman failed to understand is the nature of the "lake of fire" (Revelation 2:10,14-15). In that place of eternal damnation, the "damned" will experience profound loneliness. There will be an eternal separation of the souls, such that no one will be aware of the presence of any of their former friends or loved ones, nor of anyone else for that matter. They will have memories of them, and they will miss them terribly, but they will never again be able to enjoy their company or communicate with them in any way. Job 15:34 comments on the eternal destiny of those that have rejected God: "For the company of the godless will be barren." The woman would be remembering her husband John and longing to be with him, but all to no avail.

One day, Kay and I were spending some time with Charlotte Colmary (see Prologue). Charlotte stated that she was hoping that Barry and Julie were approving of the way in which she was caring for their twin boys.

You 'll recall from the prologue, that Barry had made arrangements with his oldest sister and her husband to become guardians of the boys, if anything ever happened to him and Julie. But, the court had not yet established the final legal authority and Sam and Charlotte were assuming the complete care of their grandsons.

As you can well imagine, this was a real labor of love. Those of us that have ever had merely one of our two-year-old grandkids for a day, know the fatigue and frustration that can set in—and the relief that comes when the parents finally arrive to reclaim the child.

Sam and Charlotte were perfect role models for grand-parenting. They displayed just the right mix of love and discipline, and the proper blending of the "nurture and admonition of the Lord."

However, mothers have their ways and grandmothers have their ways, and those "ways" don't always coincide. This was the reason for Charlotte's hope that Barry and Julie were "approving."

We tried to assure Charlotte that she was doing a magnificent job with the boys, but that, even if she were not doing it all according to either Barry's or Julie's standards, they weren't even aware of it.

Would it be heaven for them, knowing that they had left two adorable, energetic, and inquisitive, little boys behind, on Earth? I firmly believe that our Lord, in His infinite wisdom and mercy, permitted them to forget their boys—until the boys were to join their birth parents in heaven. God did, however, providentially allow Barry and Julie to take one child with them; Julie was carrying their unborn daughter in her womb when the plane crash occurred.

We often hear people say that they "know" that Dad, or a close friend, or some role model is "looking down on them from heaven." This is wishful thinking. Oh, it might be nice when we are performing well, behaving in an exemplary fashion, or have achieved some goal that those folks had encouraged use to reach to have them observe us and be proud. But what about the times when we mess up, or fail, or blow it completely? Would that be heaven for them? I think not! Job 14:21 speaks of such a man as this who has gone on to heaven: "If his sons are honored, he does not know it; if they are brought low, he does not see it."

There are many souls in heaven at this time who are giving no thought whatsoever to the horrible things that are transpiring on Earth. Their every thought is on God and the worship of Him. Their every activity is motivated by their love for God in order to bring Him glory. Their wills, their personalities, their intellect, their emotions are totally set on the triune God and His edification.

In his letter to the Colossian church, the apostle Paul encouraged them—and us—to get used to a heavenly fixation and to try not focusing so much on this world. He wrote, "Since then, you have been raised with Christ, set your hearts on things above, where Christ is seated at the right hand of God. Set your minds on things above, not on earthly things. For you died, and your life is now hidden with Christ in God" (Colossians 3:1-2).

Chapter
TWELVE

"Let Us All Sing"

When I first became a Christian, back in the early seventies, one of my greatest thrills each week was the gathering together of several local church congregations, for a "Sunday Night Sing."

A song leader would be up front asking for our favorite hymn requests, followed by some congregational singing. The four-part harmony was magnificent.

Interspersed, we would have some solos by the more talented among us, a duet or two, and a few numbers by a women's trio and a male quartet. It was a rich time of fellowship and I often thought that heaven had to be something like this.

When I've attended some good old Southern Gospel concerts, I've heard Vestal Goodman and her husband Howard speak fervently of the great days of yore when the country folk would gather on a Summer afternoon for "an all day sing and dinner on the ground." Recalling our Sunday night affairs, I could readily identify with their enthusiasm for that type of Christian fellowship.

Today, through the technology of television and VCRs, we can all enjoy Bill Gaither's recorded "Homecoming" song fests, and even sing along if we wish to—"dinner," however, is up to us.

The gathering of believers to sing has been an age-old method for the faithful to celebrate their trust in God. It's a tradition as ancient as the time of King David and his writing of the psalms.

Psalm 5:11 reads, "But let all who take refuge in you be glad; let them ever sing for joy. Spread your protection over them, that those who love your name may rejoice in you."

While psalms may have been one the first styles of music to be sung by the faithful, today we use many other musical forms in our worship services; we're encouraged to do so. The apostle Paul writes, "Speak to one another with psalms, hymns, and spiritual songs. Sing and make music in your heart to the Lord" (Ephesians 5:19).

The "spiritual songs," are those in the category of the contemporary (like Bill Gaither's). and also include the repetitive praise choruses that are common in many churches today.

Some folks like to keep the worship services more "traditional," and sing only the classical hymns, while others prefer the more contemporary style of music in their worship experience.

Of course, if one were really to be consistently "traditional" only psalms would be sung.

I have no idea what style of music we will sing in heaven, but, as one who enjoys all forms, I couldn't care less. I do know this: Everyone who sings in heaven will enjoy the music, and everyone *will* sing.

I have always enjoyed music. As a child, I'd harmonize the "old songs" with my Dad and uncles, and later, when I was in high school, I sang in a barbershop quartet. Thank God I did, for that quartet afforded me the opportunity to meet the beautiful young lady that would ultimately become my wife. Kay and I were each appearing in a variety show—she twirling a baton, and me with my quartet.

I sang with quartets in college, in medical school, and during my time in the United States Air Force. I even belonged to S.P.E.B.S.Q.S.A. (The Society for the Preservation and Encouragement of Barbershop Quartet Singing in America, Inc.).

I usually have some background music playing around the house or in my car. The "oldies" and spiritual numbers on Christian radio stations are my favorites. Music is just a very enjoyable part of my life on Earth, and I am thrilled that it will be a part of my eternal life.

I realize that not all Christians like music—at least it seems that way to me, for I often see people just standing silently at church while the rest of the congregation is singing.

Then, there are those who might like to sing, but they're tone deaf; they can't "carry a tune in a bucket."

In heaven, however, those who don't like to sing now will love it then. Those that are now tone deaf will sing on perfect pitch with their glorified vocal chords.

This heavenly singing will be one of the ways in which we will all express our joy and our thanks to God for His saving grace. Through singing we will praise, glorify, and worship Him.

In my Bible concordance—and I'm sure it's not exhaustive—there are over fifty references to singing, using words such as sing, song, sang, singer, etc. In addition, the terms music, musician, musical, etc. are referenced more than fifty times.

Finally, every Bible has the book of Psalms, a compilation of one hundred and fifty individual sets of lyrics that were set to music and sung by Old Testament and New Testament worshipers alike. Some congregations today still use the psalms exclusively during their worship in song.

In his book *The Divine Conspiracy*, Dallas Willard said this about the Psalms, "If you bury yourself in the psalms, you

87

emerge knowing God and understanding life." He was of course referring to an in-depth study of the Psalms, which I highly recommend, but singing them with understanding can have a similar effect.

The book of Revelation speaks of choirs that will be composed of both angels and glorified believers. In chapter 5 we read, "And they sang a new song: 'You are worthy to take the scroll and to open its seals, because you were slain, and with your blood you purchased men for God from every tribe and language and people and nation. You have made them to be a kingdom and priests to serve our God and they will reign on the earth'" (vv. 9-10). This song was obviously being sung to Jesus.

John continues in verses 11-12, "Then I looked and heard the voice of many angels, numbering thousands upon thousands, and ten thousand times ten thousand. They encircled the throne and the living creatures and the elders. In a loud voice they sang, 'Worthy is the Lamb, who was slain, to receive power and wealth and wisdom and strength and honor and glory and praise!'"

Did you get that? Hundreds of millions of angels are all singing—loudly. There is no stereo system that could possibly match the beauty, the tone, the volume, and the clarity (no Dolby® needed) that we will enjoy when that choir of angels starts to sing.

Continuing in verse 13, John tells of more singing, by an even larger choir. This time, we also join with them in praising the Father and the Son: "Then I heard every creature in heaven and on earth and under the earth and on the sea, and all that is in them singing: ' To Him who sits on the throne and to the Lamb be praise and honor and glory and power, forever and ever.'"

In Chapter 15, verses 2-4, John tells of another "hymn sing" going on in heaven as a special group of the redeemed sing God's praises. These are people that have been saved during the great tribulation, while the Antichrist is ruling over the earth. Their salvation experience will be truly unique, and the other saints in heaven could hardly appreciate the words they will sing.

"And I saw...those who had been victorious over the beast and his image and over the number of his name. They held harps given them by God and sang the song of Moses the servant of God and the song of the Lamb: 'Great and marvelous are your deeds, Lord Almighty. Just and true are your ways King of the ages. Who will not fear you O Lord, and bring glory to your name? For you alone are holy. All nations will come and worship before you, for your righteous acts have been revealed'" (Revelation 15:2-4).

In Revelation 14:1-3, we are told of another exclusive group that has gathered together for the express purpose of singing. They also all have something very special in common: These are the 144,000 Jewish evangelists, 12,000 from each of the twelve tribes of Israel, who were miraculously converted by God's grace and who then set out to preach the gospel of Christ during the seven years of tribulation. They each have some very unique experiences about which to sing. Here is John's account of that "song fest": "Then I looked, and there before me was the Lamb, standing on Mount Zion, and with Him 144,000 who had His name and His Father's name written on their foreheads. And I heard a sound from heaven like the roar of rushing waters and like a loud peal of thunder. The sound I heard was like that of harpists playing their harps. And they sang a new song before the throne and before the four living creatures and the elders. No one could learn the song except the 144,000 who had been redeemed from the earth."

The Lord's brother, James, asks this question in his little epistle: "Is anyone happy?" (James 5:13). Then he suggests a good way to express that sense of happiness, "Let him sing songs of praise."

In heaven we are going to experience consummate happiness, so our reasons for singing will be obvious. Singing is good for the soul. It is great therapy for those who are low in spirit. There are many reasons to sing, and every song has its own message: the message of the songwriter.

C.S. Lewis discusses this notion in his book *English Literature in the Sixteenth Century*. In it he talks of the motives behind the words of sonnet writers, and the same lesson can be applied to spiritual songwriters as well: "The sonneteers wrote not to tell their own love stories, not to express whatever in their own loves was local and peculiar, but to give us others, the inarticulate lovers, a voice. The reader was to seek in a sonnet not what the poet felt. A good sonnet was like a good public prayer: the test is whether the congregation can 'join' and make it their own, not whether it provides interesting materials for the spiritual biography of the compiler."

When we sing, in order to get the most out of the song, we need to project ourselves into it; as though it had been written exclusively for us. When we sing Spafford's "It is well with my soul," we ought to believe that our soul really is secure in Christ, for all eternity. When we sing Newton's "Amazing Grace," we should marvel at God's saving grace and be in awe over the amazing fact that He could have ever bothered to "save a wretch like me."

I have found, in my thirty-year walk with Christ, that far too many people have absolutely no idea as to the significance of what they are singing. The tunes are familiar, but the theology is somehow missing as they merely mouth the lyrics. It was in response to this that I once taught a series of Sunday school lessons on the theology that is found within the lyrics of some of our favorite old hymns. If you really want to experience a profound sense of worship while you are singing, try to decipher the meaning in each verse that you sing.

I have every confidence that heaven will be alive with singing, instrumental music, and even dancing, dancing to the music. This is certainly suggested by what we read in Psalm 149:1-5:

"Praise the LORD.
Sing to the LORD a new song,
His praise in the assembly of the saints.
Let Israel rejoice in their Maker;
let the people of Zion be glad in their King.
Let them praise His name with dancing and make music
   to Him with tambourine and harp
For the LORD takes delight in His people;
He crowns the humble with salvation.
Let the saints rejoice in His honor and sing for joy on
   their beds."

Every Sunday morning, Kay and I are privileged to be led in worship, at our church, by a sixty-voice choir, a thirty-piece orchestra, an excellent organist, a concert pianist (our pastor's wife), and so many wonderful soloists that they hardly need repeat more than twice in a year. Our minister of music has brought these musicians together in such a way that God surely "takes delight in His people."

As great as our musical format currently is, I believe that the one in heaven will far surpass its greatness. I can hardly wait for the day when the angel Gabriel lifts the trumpet to his lips and shouts, to those of us gathered around God's throne, "Let us all sing."

91

"Who's In Charge?"

*O*ne of the foremost axioms of Christian doctrine avers the absolute sovereignty of Almighty God. He is in charge. He rules the universe. "Our God is in heaven; He does whatever pleases Him" (Psalm 115:3).

R.C. Sproul, noted theologian, author, and Christian apologist, has said, "If there is one maverick molecule in the universe, God is not sovereign. And, if God is not sovereign, God is not God" (*Chosen By God*).

When Jesus ascended into heaven, forty days after His resurrection, He did so in full view of His disciples. As He rose, two angels announced that He would one day return "in the same way": bodily and visibly (Acts 1:9-11).

Christ's return to Earth is referred to as the "Second Coming" or Second Advent. He will at that time establish His earthly kingdom. When He came to Earth the first time (first advent), He came to die for our sins. He came as the "Lamb of God" (John 1:29). When He returns, He will come as the "Lion of the tribe of Judah" (Revelation 5:5), to rule as "King of Kings and Lord of Lords" (Revelation 19:16).

I happen to be in the theological camp of those who believe that Jesus' reign on earth will begin immediately following the battle of Armageddon, which brings an end to the seven year reign of the Antichrist.

Furthermore, I believe that this reign will last for one thousand years; a fact which is stressed no less than six times in the twentieth chapter of the book of Revelation.

Following Christ's millennial reign, and after a very brief Satanic rebellion (Revelation 20:7-10), God will destroy His entire created universe and replace it with "a new heaven and a new earth" (Revelation 21:1).

There are two convincing Scriptures supporting this eschatological position. The first is in Revelation 20:4, where we read, "...they came to life and reigned with Christ a thousand years." The second is Revelation 20:6, where it says, "...the second death has no power over them, but they will be priests of God and of Christ and will reign with Him for a thousand years." The "second death" refers to the spiritual death, which all unbelievers will experience in a place of eternal damnation known as "the lake of fire" (Revelation 20:14).

Regardless of your theological persuasion regarding the length of Christ's earthly reign or when it begins, the Bible clearly promises us a place in the "board room" of royal authority. The Scriptures cited above talk of our "reign" with Christ. Paul assures us of this in his second letter to Timothy, when he says, "Here is a trustworthy saying: ...we will also reign with Him" (II Timothy 2:11-12). John reaffirms this fact in Revelation 22:5, where we read, "...and they will reign forever and ever."

The book of Daniel—the Old Testament equivalent of the book of Revelation—also tells of the overthrow of the Antichrist, and the other evil earthly powers, when Christ returns. The text reads, "But the court will sit, and his power will be taken away and completely destroyed forever. Then the sovereignty, power and greatness of the kingdoms under the whole heaven will be handed over to the saints, the people of the Most High. His kingdom will be an everlasting kingdom, and all rulers will worship and obey Him" (Daniel 7:26-27).

Since many first century people were also ignorant of these facts, Paul asked this question of the Corinthian believers, "Do you not know that the saints will judge the world?" (I Corinthians 6:12).

In Romans 8:16-17, Paul writes, "The Spirit Himself testifies with our spirit that we are God's children. Now if we are children, then we are heirs, heirs of God and co-heirs with Christ, if indeed we share in His sufferings in order that we may also share in His glory."

While it is true that we will reign with Christ, there will still be a "chain of command." Several levels of increasing authority govern all orderly societies and institutions.

It practically goes without saying, that God the Father occupies the top of the cosmic organizational chart. In I Corinthians 11:3 Paul says, "Now I want you to realize that the head of every man is Christ, and the head of the woman is man, and the head of Christ is God." Thus Jesus Christ is second in command.

Jesus always asks the Father for things on our behalf (John 17:19,20), He intercedes with the Father for us (Romans 8:34), and He defends us before the Father when Satan attacks our credibility (I John 2:1). He never acts entirely on His own or apart from the will of the Father.

Jesus also tells us that He does exactly what the Father has commanded Him to do. We read of this in John 14:31: "But the world must learn that I love the Father and that I do exactly what my Father has commanded me." In John 12:49, Jesus again affirms His obedience to the Father when He says, "For I did not speak on my own accord, but the Father who sent me commanded me what to say and how to say it."

In spite of all of this, Jesus remains co-equal in power, wisdom, holiness, and most of the other characteristics attributable to God. The only one He gave up when He came to Earth the first time was His ubiquity or omnipresence. He could only be in one place at a time. Since the time of His resurrection and subsequent ascension, Jesus continues to remain limited in location. He has a body, albeit a glorified one, and for now, He occupies a position at the right hand of the Father.

The Holy Spirit, also co-equal with the Father and the Son in all respects, is third in command. In John 16:13, Jesus reminds us that the Spirit "will not speak on His own; He will speak only what He hears." What He "hears" is exactly that which the Father has told the Son. Furthermore, in John16: 14, we are told that His purpose is to "bring glory to" Jesus.

While God the Father is the "Supreme Commander," He has chosen to give "all authority in heaven and on earth" to Jesus (Matthew 28:18).

Jesus, in turn, will delegate some of His rule to the twelve apostles. We read of this in Luke 22:28-30: "You are those who have stood by me in my trials. And I confer on you a kingdom, just as my Father conferred one on me, so that you may eat and drink at my table in the kingdom and sit on thrones, judging the twelve tribes of Israel."

Next in the chain of command are all the saints: all of the believers of all time, from Adam, Eve, and Abel to the last soul saved by the grace of God. Now, you might be thinking, who could possibly remain to be under our authority?

During the millennial reign, there will be unbelievers on Earth. They will be those unregenerate people who persist following the battle of Armageddon, which takes place only in the Middle East. These people will inhabit the other parts of Earth and may possibly number in the billions.

They will be in total submission to us, because the evil power that now controls them will be chained and locked up during this time. Revelation 20:1-3 reads, "And I saw an angel coming down out of heaven...holding in his hand a great chain. He seized the dragon, that ancient serpent, which is the devil, or Satan, and bound him for a thousand years. He threw him into the Abyss, and locked and sealed it over him, to keep him from deceiving the nations anymore until the thousand years were ended. After that, he must be set free for a short time."

These earthly citizens will no longer be following Satan's orders, for he will have no capacity to be "at work in them" (Ephesians 2:1-3) or deceiving them.

During this time, they will appear to be very moral, kind, passive, humble, generous, and loving people. However, as soon as Satan is released from his chains, their true colors will be shown. We read of this change in attitude and behavior in Revelation 20:7-10: "When the thousand years are over, Satan will be released from his prison and will go out to deceive the nations in the Four Corners of the earth...to gather them for battle. In number they are like the sand on the seashore. They marched across the breadth of the earth and surrounded the camp of God's people, the city He loves. But fire came down from heaven and devoured them. And the devil, who deceived them, was thrown into the lake of burning sulfur, where the beast and the false prophet had been thrown. They will be tormented day and night for ever and ever."

Now you might be thinking, "Alright, that takes care of the 'reign' question on Earth, but when we are in heaven, where there will be no unbelievers, over whom will we reign?" The answer to that question is found in I Corinthians 6:3, where Paul says, "Do you not know that we will judge angels?"

As pointed out in Chapter Five, there will be millions of angels residing there with us. Surprisingly, as powerful as they are, they will be under our command. Angels have, since their creation, been in heaven to serve the Father, and they will ultimately also be serving us.

As a matter of fact, since the day that we were born, each one of the elect, the chosen people of God, has had a guardian angel, standing by to protect and serve. Hebrews 1:14 is proof of this: "Are not all angels ministering spirits sent to serve those who will inherit salvation?" In Psalm 91:11 we read that

God "...will command His angels concerning you to guard you in all your ways."

Note that the verse in Hebrews reads, "those who *will* inherit salvation." That means future believers, even before they begin to believe.

Some of you may now be thinking that being in charge will produce a bunch of folks with "swelled heads"and "puffed up" egos. Not so! As we shall see in the next chapter, in our glorified state of existence our propensity for prideful feelings will be absent and we will have the mind of Christ. Of course, this is also the kind of attitude that we should now be developing through the process of progressive sanctification. Paul encouraged this in Philippians 2:5-7 where he wrote,"Your attitude should be the same as that of Christ Jesus: Who being in very nature God, did not consider equality with God something to be grasped, but made Himself nothing, taking the very nature of a servant, being found in human likeness."

In heaven, we will be totally content with our place in the cosmic chain of command. We won't envy the apostles above us, and we won't look condescendingly on the angels below. The purpose of the chain of command is to maintain order in heaven, for it has always been God's desire that "everything should be done in a fitting and orderly way" (I Corinthians 14:40).

Relationships

One of the most frequently asked questions regarding relationships in heaven is, "Will my spouse and I still be married?" I can wholeheartedly understand the concern of any Christian that asks that question. Anyone who has had a wonderful, loving, and fulfilling marital relationship here on Earth would surely hope that it might continue on into eternity.

My wife Kay is my companion, my confidant, my encourager, my lover, my greatest critic, and my best friend. There is no one else on earth with whom I would rather spend eternity, and to whom I would rather be married in heaven, if that were possible. But that is just not the way it is going to be. Heaven will be devoid of the human, earthly, man-woman, marriage relationship.

Jesus clears this issue up very succinctly in Matthew 22:23-30: "The same day the Sadducees, who say there is no resurrection, came to Him with a question. 'Teacher,' they said, 'Moses told us that if a man dies without having children, his brother must marry the widow and have children for him. Now there were seven brothers among us. The first one married and died, and since he had no children, he left his wife to his brother. The same thing happened to the second and third brother, right on down to the seventh. Finally the woman died. Now then, at the resurrection, whose wife will she be of the seven, since all of them were married to her?' Jesus replied, 'You are in error because you do not know the scriptures or the power of God. At the resurrection people will neither marry nor be given in marriage; they will be like the angels in heaven.'"

If that surprises you, you are not alone, for the 33rd verse of that same chapter in Matthew says, "When the crowds heard this, they were astonished at His teaching."

We are currently thinking as earthly people, Christians who are merely living in a spiritual state of justification and partial sanctification, thus it is quite natural for us to want our heavenly relationships to mirror those on earth. However, in heaven we will be in a state of glorification, and that is a supernatural state. Thus our thinking will be entirely transformed.

Before we were "born again," or regenerated, and spiritually dead to the things of God, we had an ungodly worldview. We considered the Christian life to be dull, restrictive, unfulfilling, and rigorous. However, having been made new by the Spirit of God, we came to believe otherwise. Now, looking back, we can't imagine living without the presence and influence of Christ, His Spirit, and His Word in our lives. We've experienced a "renewing" of our minds (Romans 12:2), and we are "new creatures" in Christ (II Corinthians 5:17).

Just as there is now a vivid contrast between our new mindset and the old, between the regenerate and the unregenerate, there will be an even more drastic change in our heavenly, glorified frame of mind.

A good marriage is the closest thing to heaven that a believer will ever experience on earth. It is the pattern that God has established, and it symbolizes our everlasting relationship with Christ.

In Ephesians 5:22-28, 31-32, the Scriptures intermingle the earthly marriage of husbands and wives with the heavenly marriage of Christ and His church: "Wives submit yourselves to your husbands *as to the Lord*. For the husband is the head of the wife *as Christ is the head of the church, His body, of which He is the Savior. Now as the church submits to Christ,* so also wives should submit to their husbands in everything. Husbands, love your wives, *just as Christ loved the church and gave Himself up for her to make her holy, cleansing her by the washing with water through the word, and to present her to Himself as a radiant church, without stain or wrinkle or any other blemish, but holy and blameless.* In this same way, husbands ought to love their wives as their own bodies. He who loves his wife loves himself. '…For this reason a man will leave his father and mother and be united to his wife, and the two will become one flesh.' This is a profound mystery…but *I am talking about Christ and the church*" (emphasis added; these portions reflect the Christ/church relationship).

Jesus refers to Himself as our bridegroom (Matthew 25:1,5), and the church is called His bride (Revelation 19:5; 21:2,9; 22:17). Our wedding ceremony and reception are also discussed in Revelation 19:7-8.

Finally, in making this point, the prophet Isaiah talks of God's marriage relationship with us in Isaiah 62:5: "…as a bridegroom rejoices over his bride, so will your God rejoice over you."

I'm counting on the fact that my relationship with Kay, as great as it now is, will be even better in heaven, and that my relationship with the "bridegroom," my Lord and Savior Jesus Christ, will surpass even that.

In addition to relating to our Lord, and to our spouses (assuming that they, too, are Christians), heaven will be replete with redeemed souls from ages past and from all of the nations on earth. Furthermore, our relationship with these people will be perfect.

It is Jesus' desire that Christians "...love the Lord your God with all your heart and with all your soul and with all your mind," and that we should "...love your neighbor as yourself" (Matthew 22:37,39).

In heaven there will be no generation gap. We'll be living with people who walked the earth thousands of years ago. Somehow, and I don't understand how, our glorified bodies will not show our age differentials. Adam, Eve, Abel, Enoch, and Noah will all look the same age as Peter and Paul, even though they lived thousands of years apart. We in turn will look the same age as every other saint from all time.

There will be a universal, heavenly, common language spoken there, just as there was before God "confused" the language at the tower of Babel (Genesis 11:1-9). Thus we will be able to communicate with believers from every age and culture from the beginning of time.

There will also be no gender gap or racial prejudice. Paul expressed this notion in his letter to the church in Galatia, which was having a problem with prejudice, when he wrote, "You are all sons of God through faith in Christ Jesus. For all of you who were baptized into Christ have clothed yourselves with Christ. There is neither Jew nor Greek, slave nor free, male nor female, for you all are one in Christ Jesus. If you belong to Christ, then you are Abraham's seed, and heirs according to the promise."

Since our sinful, corruptible natures will have been left behind, and we will have attained a state of perfect righteousness and holiness "just like Jesus," we will never again express, "hatred, discord, jealousy, fits of rage, selfish ambition, dissention, factions, and envy" (Galatians 5:20-21).

No one will gossip, backbite, or quarrel. We will possess an entirely new demeanor. We will have the mind of Christ.

James, the brother of our Lord, talks about the nature we will leave behind as he poses a question and then immediately answers it: "What causes fights and quarrels among you? Don't they come from your desires that battle within you?

101

You want something but don't get it. You kill, and covet, but you cannot have what you want. You quarrel and fight..." (James 4:1-2).

We will be friends with everyone, because we will be united with one purpose and one desire—to glorify and enjoy our triune God forever.

Paul pleaded with the Ephesian church, and us, to "make every effort to keep the unity of the Spirit in the bond of peace" (Ephesians 4:3).

In heaven, expressing love and living in peace will be effortless. It will be our "supernatural" inclination. We will enjoy perfect Christian fellowship; the Greek word is *koinonia*. Theological distinctions will be gone. We will have a common theology, and it will be correct in every way.

Chapter
FIFTEEN

"What Will We Know?"

*T*he apostle Paul was a brilliant man, and one of the greatest apologists that the church has ever had. But even Paul was, admittedly, limited in his knowledge. He stated this clearly in his first letter to the church at Corinth: "Now we see but a poor reflection as in a mirror, then we shall see face to face. Now I know in part; then I shall know fully, even as I am fully known" (I Corinthians 13:12).

At this point in time, we have been given all of the spiritual information that God wants us to have. That information is found within the pages of His Word, the Holy Bible. There is much however, that remains a mystery. Moses told the people of Israel, and us, that "the secret things belong to the Lord our God, but the things revealed belong to us and to our children forever, that we may follow all the words of this law" (Deuteronomy 29:29).

In heaven, some of that voluminous information, that is now referred to as "secret things," will be revealed to us. Our knowledge base will have increased tremendously.

Jesus told His disciples, "I have much more to say to you, more than you can now bear. But when He, the Spirit of Truth comes, He will guide you into all Truth" (John 16:12-13). Without the Holy Spirit, Jesus' words have always fallen on "deaf" ears. Until our "ears" are glorified, and we have entered heaven, the additional information that He has to "say" would be incomprehensible. Some of the secrets of God are currently too much for us to bear. They would literally "blow our minds."

There are basically three levels of capacity when it comes to knowledge. There is the capacity for worldly knowledge, for spiritual knowledge, and for heavenly knowledge.

Worldly knowledge will differ, based upon a person's intellectual aptitude (I.Q.), the desire to learn and apply that aptitude, and one's educational opportunities (i.e., the level attained in the various institutions of learning).

Spiritual knowledge, that which is gained from God concerning His kingdom, is utterly dependent upon our being "born again" and indwelt by the Holy Spirit. Jesus said, "I tell you the truth, no one can see the kingdom of God unless he is born again" (John 3:3). The word "see" there means to comprehend or understand.

In I Corinthians 2:12-14 Paul further explains this: "We have not received the spirit of the world but the Spirit who is from God, that we may understand what God has freely given us. This is what we speak, not in words taught us by human wisdom but in words taught by the Spirit, expressing spiritual truths in spiritual words. The man without the Spirit does not accept the things that come from the Spirit of God, for they are foolishness to him and he cannot understand them because they are spiritually discerned." Notice that it reads "he cannot understand" spiritual truths. This is not a matter of the will, but of capability.

Heavenly knowledge will surpass all human knowledge, both worldly and spiritual. Albert Einstein, one of the greatest minds of the twentieth century, is reported to have said that he knew only three percent of all there is to know. In heaven, we will have the capacity to know the other ninety-seven percent.

King Solomon was, reportedly, the most intelligent man that ever lived. He asked God for wisdom and God answered, "I will do what you have asked. I will give you a wise and discerning heart, so that there will never have been anyone like you, nor will there ever be" (I kings 3:12).

In I Kings 4:29-34, the Bible details Solomon's intellectual capacity: "God gave Solomon wisdom and very great insight, and a breadth of understanding as measureless as the sand on the seashore. Solomon's wisdom was greater than the wisdom of all the men of the East, and greater than all the wisdom of Egypt. He was wiser than any other man.... And his fame spread to all the surrounding nations. He spoke three thousand proverbs and his songs numbered a thousand and five. He described plant life, from the cedars of Lebanon to the hyssop that grows out of walls. He also taught about animals and birds, reptiles and fish. Men of all nations came to listen to Solomon's wisdom, sent by all the kings of the world, who had heard of his wisdom."

Just think, Solomon could have taught in any of our universities and his professorial skills would have included philosophy, music, botany, zoology, ornithology, herpetology, and marine biology.

As great an intelligence as Solomon possessed, and as great as our knowledge base will be, God's will be greater still.

God is omniscient. He knows everything that has happened, that is happening, and that will happen. Furthermore, He knows all of the things that could have happened, but didn't—all of the possibilities. Writing in the devotional *Tabletalk* (Ligonier Ministries), R.C. Sproul put it this way, "God knows all contingencies but not contingently."

The Bible tells us these things about God's knowledge base: "Can anyone teach knowledge to God, since He judges even the highest?" (Job 21:22); "Who has understood the mind of the Lord, or instructed Him as His counselor? Whom did the Lord consult to enlighten Him, and who taught Him the right way? Who was it that taught Him knowledge or showed Him the path of understanding?" (Isaiah 40:13-14); "I make known the end from the beginning, from ancient times, what is still to come" (Isaiah 46:10); "Oh, the depth of the riches of the wisdom and knowledge of God! How unsearchable His judgements, and His paths beyond tracing out!" (Romans 11:33).

In heaven, our capacity for insight, understanding, wisdom, and knowledge, though great, will still be finite. Only God is infinite, and the finite can never fully comprehend nor equal the infinite.

David spoke of his limited capacity to understand the things of God, when he said, "Such knowledge is too wonderful for me, too lofty for me to attain" (Psalm 139:6). Now, however, David is in heaven where his ability to understand the "wonderful" and the "lofty" has been greatly magnified. Yet, as expanded as David's mind has become, it still pales when compared to the mind of God.

Proverbs 1:7 reads, "The fear of the Lord is the beginning of knowledge." That refers to the "spiritual" and the "heavenly" knowledge explained above. Worldly knowledge began with our physical birth; spiritual knowledge and heavenly knowledge depend upon our spiritual birth. What was initiated with our walk of faith, will be completed in heaven.

We will have to await our glorification to attain the heavenly capacity for knowledge, but, for now, our capacity to gain spiritual knowledge is limited only by our own degree of tenacity, discipline, and faithfulness in searching the Scriptures.

David discovered this fact and thus wrote, "Oh, how I love your law! I meditate on it all day long. Your commands make me wiser than my enemies, for they are ever with me. I have more insight than all my teachers, for I meditate on your statutes. I have more understanding than the elders, for I obey your precepts" (Psalm 119:97-100).

The words "law," "commands," and "precepts" are synonyms for the Bible. Note that he twice mentioned meditating on it. That means he diligently studied God's Word. Note also that it was "ever with" him. He kept it handy for quick reference and study. Most importantly, David said that he obeyed what he had learned from God's Word. He put it into practice. As a result David gained wisdom, insight, and understanding. If you and I are diligent to do the same, we will also gain a tremendous amount of spiritual knowledge.

Many of us have great thirsts for knowledge; we read, we study, we view the "History Channel," we search the Internet, and we discuss a great many things with great numbers of people. When we get to heaven, that thirst for information will be entirely satisfied, and our heavenly capacity for knowledge will be filled.

Chapter
SIXTEEN

The Soul

We humans have been created in the image of God (Genesis 1:26; 9:6), and this is what sets us apart from all other living creatures. God has made us like Himself. And yet, we are told that God is a Spirit (John 4:24). God doesn't have a body. Thus, the resemblance between God and man must reside somewhere other than within our physical nature. In fact, it does: it resides in the soul.

When we study the attributes of God, we find certain things in common with man.

Man is *rational*. God implies this in Isaiah 1:18, where He says, "Come now let us reason together." If man were irrational, he could not reason with God or anyone else for that matter.

Our rational minds permit us to contemplate, to cogitate, to calculate, to plan, to reason, and to doubt.

Man is *moral*. Even the pagan knows right from wrong. Romans 2:14-15 reads, "Indeed, when the Gentiles, who do not have the law, do by nature the things required by the law, they are a law for themselves, even though they do not have the law, since they show that the requirements of the law are written on their hearts, their consciences also bearing witness, and their thoughts now accusing, now even defending them."

Every culture that has ever existed on earth has had a moral code or ethical underpinning. Also, the most ignorant of humans, in the remotest areas of the globe, are aware of some "higher power" to whom they sense they are answerable.

Man is *personal*. We express emotion. We love, we hate, we grieve, and we rejoice. God is said to do all of these things. He loves (John 3:16), He hates (Psalm 5:5), He grieves (Genesis 6:6), and He rejoices (Isaiah 62:5). This is because God too is personal.

Man is *volitional*. He has a will. Jonathan Edwards has defined the will as "the mind choosing" (*The Rational Biblical Theology of Jonathan Edwards, Volume II*).

Man was created with a free will. Adam and Eve had the moral ability to choose the good or the bad, to obey or disobey God's only commandment. They chose to disobey, and, in doing so, ironically, they lost the ability to choose the right. Ever since the Fall, every human that has ever been born, has lacked the capacity to choose the "good," as defined by God (Genesis 6:5; 8:21; Romans 3:11-12). While it is true, that even in our unregenerate state, we did some good or decent things, we did not yet possess the capacity for doing the things that would lead us to salvation or acceptance by God. When we have been born again, the ability to choose the good and the right way is restored to us. Having been bound by sin, Christ sets us free (John 8:32,36). He frees our wills from their bondage to sin and enables us to do what is pleasing to God.

God also has a will, and this is stated over and over again in the Bible; Luke 22:42 and I Peter 3:17 are just two of these references.

Man is *industrious*. In Genesis 2:2, we find that God placed Adam in the Garden of Eden to "work." The need to work has been erroneously attributed to the fall, as a part of the curse.

The statement about work in Genesis 2 precedes the fall, which is described in Genesis 3. Work need not be onerous. It can be a blessing when approached with the proper attitude.

God too is always at work, directing and sustaining the universe (Colossians 1:17) and working in the hearts of believers (Romans 8:28; Philippians 1:6).

Man is *intelligent*. While God is the source of all intelligence and is Himself omniscient, He has given varying degrees of intellectual capacity to man.

Man is *creative*. God's other creatures are programmed to do the things they do. They are not intuitive, they are not inventive, and they are not original. They are not free to create new ways of doing things, except in rare cases of adaptation. They always do what they are supposed to do. For example, a bee always makes hexagonal cells for its honeycomb; spiders of specific subspecies spin webs characteristic of their particular grouping; beavers build very similar dams; and birds of the same "feather" make unique kinds of nests, each according to a previously prescribed design.

Mankind has been able to harness the powers of nature—through his inventiveness, through her creativity. Man has been endowed with the ability to improve his lifestyle through his creative intelligence.

It is the soul that is the seat of all of the above human attributes. It is the soul that will go to heaven when our physical life is over. The soul is the real "us." The soul defines who we are.

The body is merely a temporary repository or residence for the soul. The body is the vehicle that gets the soul from point A to point B. The body, via its five senses, enables us to communicate with the physical world around us. The soul makes it possible for us to relate to one another.

Both Paul and Peter make this distinction in their writings, and each calls the body a "tent" for the soul.

First we read from Paul: "Now we know that if the earthly tent we live in is destroyed, we have a building from God, an eternal house in heaven, not built by human hands. Meanwhile we groan, longing to be clothed in our heavenly dwelling, because when we are clothed, we will not be found naked. For while we are in this tent we groan and are burdened, because we do not wish to be unclothed but to be clothed with our heavenly dwelling, so that what is mortal may be swallowed up with life" (II Corinthians 5:1-4). The body is mortal; the soul is life eternal.

It is interesting to note Paul's use of the words "naked," "unclothed," and "clothed." He says that we humans "wish...to be clothed." I believe that this refers back to the shame that Adam and Eve experienced immediately following their sin against God. Genesis 3:7 reads,"Then the eyes of both of them were opened, and they realized they were naked; so they sewed fig leaves together and made coverings for themselves." In heaven, we will have no reason to be ashamed of anything, and we secretly long for that.

And now we quote Peter: "I think it is right to refresh your memory as long as I live in the tent of this body, because I know that I will soon put it aside as our Lord Jesus Christ has made clear to me" (II Peter 1:13-14).

When Peter says "I will put it aside," he means that his body and soul will separate; his body will return to the ground and his soul to God. As Solomon states in Ecclesiastes 12:7, "...the dust returns to the ground it came from, and the spirit returns to God who gave it." Here "spirit" is synonymous with soul.

There is a part of our soul that is dormant, or "dead," at birth. Ephesians 2:1,4 tells us that we were "dead" in sin. This means spiritually dead. At some later time during our physical life, by God's grace, He "makes us alive" and we are born again.

Unless that happens, upon one's physical death the soul will depart to Hell, where it will reside in utter torment eternally.

There is a saying, common among Christians, that is apropos here: "If you are born twice, you die once. If your are born once, you die twice." What that means is this: If you have been born physically, but not spiritually, you will live in a place of eternal damnation, which is not "life" at all; if, however, you have been born again, anew, from above, spiritually, you will merely experience a physical death, following which your soul will immediately depart to live with God in the third heaven eternally. Jesus put it this way, "I tell you the truth, no one can enter the kingdom of God unless he is born of water and the Spirit" (John 3:5). The water (i.e., amniotic fluid) birth that Jesus refers to is physical and the Spirit birth is spiritual, being born again.

If you want your soul to go to heaven when your body dies, "You must be born again" (John 3:3). When your physical life has come to an end, if you have become a Christian, your soul will immediately go to heaven. I would urge you to get ready for a sudden departure!

Chapter
SEVENTEEN

Now the Rewards

*T*he *World Book Dictionary* defines a reward as "a payment for something done." Heaven itself is not to be
considered a reward, because there is absolutely *nothing* that
you or I can do to deserve heaven. Heaven, and the eternal life
that we will enjoy there, is exclusively a gift from God. It is
free to us, but it was not free. Jesus paid the ultimate price for
our eternal life: His own life.

The Bible says, "No man can redeem the life of another or
give to God a ransom for him—the ransom for a life is costly,
no payment is ever enough" (Psalm 49:7-8). While that is
obviously true, Jesus, who did redeem us and who did give
God a ransom for our lives, was not just a man. Jesus was very
(truly) God and very (truly) man. He was as much divine as
He was human.

Our salvation is a free gift; of this there can be no doubt. It's
not a "payment for something done," because we didn't do anything to receive it. Ephesians 2:8-9 reads, "For it is by grace you
have been saved, through faith—and this not from yourselves,
it is the gift of God—not by works, so that no one can boast."

Reading on however, in verse 10, we find that we are saved to "do" good works: "For we are God's workmanship, created in Christ Jesus to *do* good works, which God prepared in advance for us to *do*" (emphasis added).

The Christian life is about doing good. Furthermore, the things that we should be doing have been foreordained by God, "prepared in advance."

In order to accomplish these works, God has equipped each Christian with one or more spiritual gifts (Romans 12:6-8; I Corinthians 12:1-11; Ephesians 4:8-13).

We are told, "Each one should use whatever gift he has received to serve others, faithfully administering God's grace in its various forms" (I Peter 4:10).

Though heaven itself is not a "reward," we will be receiving rewards in heaven. When we arrive there, immediately upon our physical demise, "...we must all appear before the judgment seat of Christ, that each one may receive what is due him for the things done while in the body, whether good or bad" (II Corinthians 5:10).

It is at this "judgment seat of Christ," that our works will be judged. We will be called upon to give an account of how faithfully we used our spiritual gifts and how diligently we accomplished those foreordained works for which God has saved us. This is not a judgment seat for sin. There will be no mention of past sin here, for our sin was dealt with at the Cross of Calvary where Jesus "bore the sin of many" (Isaiah 53:12). Furthermore, God has assured all believers that he will "remember their sins no more" (Jeremiah 31:34).

God will reward us for accomplishing the tasks for which we have been gifted. There are also many areas of common or collective responsibility for which we will receive rewards, if we have been faithful in carrying them out.

One of these responsibilities for believers is to bear up under the scorn of unbelievers. Jesus said, "Blessed are you when men hate you, when they exclude you and insult you and reject your name as evil because of the Son of Man.

Rejoice in that day and leap for joy, because great is your reward in heaven..." (Luke 6:22-23). Thus the more "flack" that we take while here on Earth because of our faith in Christ, the greater the reward we'll receive in heaven.

Soul winning will also be rewarded. You and I may not see the final results of our witness while we're here on earth, but each "seed" of faith that we have sown, that which subsequently brings forth the "fruit of righteousness" will result in a reward. We are assured that "...he who sows righteousness reaps a sure reward" (Proverbs 11:18). That is why we are told in Proverbs 11:30, that "...he who wins souls is wise." Won't it be thrilling to meet some person in heaven that credits you with bringing him or her to the knowledge of Christ?

Supporting charitable organizations, especially those that minister to the poor and homeless (Salvation Army, Rescue Missions, etc.), will be rewarded. "He who is kind to the poor lends to the LORD, and He will reward him for what he has done" (Proverbs 19:17).

There are many other ways to serve our Lord, and each of us is expected to do so. That service does not go unnoticed by God, and He is keeping a record of our good works. Paul says that being a faithful employee in one's place of business is itself deserving of a reward. "Serve wholeheartedly, as if you were serving the Lord, not men, because you know that the Lord will reward everyone for whatever good he does..." (Ephesians 6:7-8).

Many Christians and Old Testament believers throughout history have lost everything, including their lives, for their faith in God. Just recently, a deranged young killer gunned down a young lady at Columbine High School in Littleton, Colorado, because she would not denounce her faith in Christ.

The Bible is replete with accounts of martyrs who suffered because of their faith—from Abel (Genesis 4:8), to the apostle John (Revelation 1:9), to the saints that will be beheaded during the tribulation (Revelation 20:4).

The book of Hebrews summarizes some of the experiences of the elect "who through faith conquered kingdoms, administered justice, and gained what was promised; who shut the mouths of lions, quenched the fury of the flames, and escaped the edge of the sword; whose weakness was turned to strength; and who became powerful in battle and routed foreign armies. Women received back their dead, raised to life again. Others were tortured and refused to be released, so that they might gain a better resurrection. Some faced jeers and flogging, while still others were chained and put in prison. They were stoned; they were sawed in two; they were put to death by the sword. They went about in sheepskins and goatskins, destitute, persecuted and mistreated— the world was not worthy of them. They wandered in deserts and mountains, and in caves and holes in the ground" (Hebrews 11:33-38).

These believers will not go unrewarded for their martyrdom. The author of Hebrews tells of their rewards: "Remember those earlier days after you had received the light, when you stood your ground in a great contest in the face of suffering. Sometimes you were publicly exposed to insult and persecution; at other times you stood side by side with those who were so treated. You sympathized with those in prison and joyfully accepted the confiscation of your property, because you knew that you yourselves had better and lasting possessions. So do not throw away your confidence; it will be richly rewarded. You need to persevere so that when you have done the will of God, you will receive what He has promised" (Hebrews 10:32-36).

I have no idea just what form these various rewards will all take, but the Bible does speak of different kinds of crowns.

Revelation 4:4,10 tells of golden crowns, worn by a group of "twenty-four elders." Some Bible scholars think that these two dozen people represent twelve leaders from the twelve tribes of "true" or faithful Israel plus the twelve apostles (remember, they are to be just below Jesus, in the chain of

116

command; see Chapter Thirteen). That speculative identity may or may not be true, but these twenty-four elders must be very special persons to be honored in this way.

Each believer will receive a "crown of life," signifying their free gift of eternal life (Revelation 2:10; James 1:12), but, as pointed out above, this is not a reward because it is not earned.

The apostle Peter speaks of a "crown of glory" (I Peter 5:4). This testifies to the final step in our transition from justification, through progressive sanctification, and finally glorification. This too cannot be considered a reward, since our glorification, like our justification, is purely a work of God.

Paul mentions a "crown of righteousness" in II Timothy 4:8. This will probably compliment our robe of righteousness, and together they are signs that we have been faithful to committing "righteous acts" (i.e., good works) while on earth, following our experience of salvation (Revelation 19:8).

The rewards that we sometimes get on Earth are temporal, and trivial in comparison to those that we will receive in heaven, for these are eternal. In I Corinthians 9 the apostle Paul puts earthly rewards into their proper perspective: "Do you not know that in a race all the runners run, but only one gets the prize? Everyone who competes in the games goes into strict training. They do it to get a crown that will not last; but we do it to get a crown that will last forever" (vv. 24-25).

Paul had obviously been a sports fan, and had enjoyed watching the ancient Olympic Games in Athens, Greece. Because of his interest in athletic endeavors he was aware of the agonies that each of these athletes went through to win a small gold leafed crown. He also knew that Christians too would lead rigorous lives—some more rigorous than others would—by living out their faith and striving against a hostile world for the cause of Christ. The difference would be in the reward. The Olympic crown was temporal, while the crown of life is eternal.

EIGHTEEN

"What's For Dinner?"

*I*f there is one non-spiritual activity that Christians most enjoy doing together, it's eating. Whenever I recall my childhood and being at the church for any reason other than worship, it was to eat at a "covered dish dinner" in the Fellowship Hall.

It was said of the first century Christians that they "ate together with glad and sincere hearts" (Acts 2:46). We are still doing that! Thank God for "covered dish dinners." And I'm glad to report that we'll also be enjoying fellowship meals together in heaven. You see, even glorified bodies can enjoy food.

When Jesus appeared to His disciples after the resurrection (in His glorified body), He asked, "Do you have anything here to eat?" Then in response to His question, we read that they "gave Him a piece of broiled fish, and He took it and ate it in their presence" (Luke 24:41-43).

When we have gone to heaven, and have been married to our "bridegroom," Jesus Christ, we will all celebrate the occasion with a wedding supper. We know this from the passage in Revelation 19:9, which reads, "...Blessed are those who are invited to the wedding supper of the Lamb...." Since we, the church, the body of believers, are called the "bride" of Christ, we will certainly be among those who receive invitations. God has already sent in an RSVP for each believer, marked: "yes."

The "bill of fare" for this meal is found delineated in Isaiah 25:6: "...The LORD Almighty will prepare a feast of rich food for all peoples, a banquet of aged wine—the best of meats and the finest of wines."

No hamburger or hotdogs for us just filet mignon, prime rib of beef, pork loin, and pheasant under glass. No cheap wines either. Only the "gold medal" winners from the Napa Valley and the vineyards of Italy and France.

I know what some of you are thinking: drinking wine is a sin. If that is true—and it isn't—then you are accusing Jesus of sin.

Remember that His first miracle was the turning of water into wine—wine not grape juice. It wasn't that someone had forgotten to buy wine for the wedding reception. The problem was clearly stated by the apostle John who wrote, "When the wine was gone, Jesus' mother said to Him, 'They have no more wine'" (John 2:3). If Jesus had disapproved of their libations He could have arrived a bit earlier and performed an equally impressive miracle of turning all of their wine into water.

In my early years as a Christian, I was taught that Jesus had turned the water into grape juice. Later however, I learned that the Greek word for wine, used in John chapter 2, is *oinos*. This same usage is expressed in Ephesians 5:18 where we are warned not to get drunk with wine (*oinos*). It's fairly evident that you can't get drunk on grape juice.

At the Last Supper, the cup was filled with wine (*oinos*). Jesus told His disciples that He would not drink wine again with them until "the kingdom of God comes" (Luke 22:18). He was obviously referring to heaven.

Psalm 104:15 tells us that God has provided "wine that gladdens the heart of man." That is true in more than just an emotional sense. Medical research has proven that a glass of red wine each day improves one's cholesterol profile; it lowers LDL ("bad" cholesterol) and raises HDL ("good" cholesterol). I know this first hand, because I have suggested it to my patients and seen it work. Furthermore, a statistical analysis of deaths from myocardial infarction reveals a surprisingly higher mortality rate among teetotalers.

There is absolutely no harm in abstaining from alcoholic beverages or, for that matter, from any other food. It's purely a matter of personal preference. There will not be any reward in heaven for either practice.

Vegetarians, avoiding meat for various reasons, will obviously have lower serum cholesterols, and thus suffer fewer heart attacks and strokes. That practice gains some earthly rewards but does not qualify for any accolades in heaven. As a matter of fact, all humans were vegetarians prior to the flood (Genesis 3:29 and 9:3). This is what, in part, accounted for their longevity.

Both wines and meats (especially fat-laden kinds) can be abused to the point of endangering one's health. Obesity, for example, is exceeded only by tobacco as the leading cause of preventable death in the United States. The devastating effects of alcohol abuse are well known to us all. On the other hand, the prudent partaking of foods, including wine (wine is also listed as a food in God's Word: Haggai 2:12), is not included among the numerous biblical lists of sins. Judging is, however.

On at least three occasions, the Bible declares some medicinal value in alcoholic beverages.

Proverbs 31:6 reads, "Give beer to those who are perishing, wine to those who are in anguish." Thus we see that in times past, God had recommended these substances as a comfort measure in the terminally ill; much the same as we now use morphine and other narcotics. Furthermore, alcoholic drinks were to be used as a sedative to relieve anxiety.

In I Timothy 5:23, Paul advised his sickly friend Timothy to "stop drinking only water, and use a little wine because of your stomach and your frequent illnesses."

In Luke 10:34, Jesus tells of a Good Samaritan man who found another man "half dead" from a beating. The Samaritan bandaged his wounds and poured "on oil and wine." The oil was no doubt soothing, and prevented the bandages from sticking to the wounds, whereas the wine, with its alcohol content, provided some antisepsis.

Wine, like atomic energy, is only bad when it is placed in the wrong hands and used for the wrong purposes.

I have found that abstinence is based more on tradition than on biblical imperatives. A perfect example of this fact is found in Jeremiah 35:1-16: "This is the word that came to Jeremiah from the LORD during the reign of Jehoiakim son of Josiah king of Judah: 'Go to the Recabite family and invite them to come to one of the side rooms of the house of the LORD and give them wine to drink.'

"So I went to get Jaazaniah son of Jeremiah, the son of Habazziniah, and his brothers and all his sons—the whole family of the Recabites. I brought them into the house of the LORD, into the room of the sons of Hanan son of Igdaliah the man of God. It was next to the room of the officials, which was over that of Maaseaih son of Shallum the doorkeeper. Then I set bowls full of wine and some cups before the men of the Recabite family and said to them, 'Drink some wine.'

"But they replied, 'We do not drink wine, because our forefather Jonadab son of Recab gave us this command: "Neither you nor your descendants must ever drink wine. Also you must never build houses, sow seed or plant vineyards; you must never have any of these things, but must always live in tents. Then you will live a long time in the land where you are nomads." We have obeyed everything our forefather Jonadab son of Recab commanded us. Neither we nor our wives nor our sons and daughters have ever drunk wine or built houses to live in or had vineyards, fields, or crops. We have lived in tents and have fully obeyed everything our father Jonadab commanded us.'"

Thus far we see a tradition building here: a tradition of abject legalism. Nowhere had God commanded this family to place any of these restrictions on themselves. Yet, it is obvious that they felt very pious, very "spiritual," for doing so.

Jesus warned about such a "piety" in Matthew chapter 23 as He condemned the Pharisees for their religiosity.

We continue on in verses 12-16: "The word of the LORD came to Jeremiah, saying, 'this is what the LORD Almighty, the God of Israel, says: Go tell the men of Judah and the people of Jerusalem, 'Will you not learn a lesson and obey my words?' declares the LORD. 'Jonadab son of Recab ordered his sons not to drink wine and this command has been kept. To this day they do not drink wine, because they obey their forefather's command. But I have spoken to you again and again, yet you have not obeyed me.'"

The lesson here is not that family traditions are bad. Whatever restrictions families—such as the Recabites—choose to place upon themselves is really a matter of personal preference.

What God is saying to the citizens of Jerusalem is this: "I have given you many laws in my Word that I consider significant, and of eternal consequence, but you have failed to follow them." God has placed enough restrictions upon us, and has instructed us regarding our behavior in countless ways. Love your neighbors; don't gossip; don't lie. don't lust; pray without ceasing; study the Word of God, etc., etc., etc.

There is no need for us to add to them. Our main purpose, as Christians, is to "...Fear God and keep His commandments, for this is the whole duty of man" (Ecclesiastes 12:13). Regardless of one's preference or tradition while here on Earth, both meat and wine will be on the menu in heaven.

I'm a bit saddened, however, by the implication that we won't be enjoying any good seafood: no lobster, crab legs, oysters, crab cakes, stuffed flounder, Lake Superior whitefish, or Great Lakes walleye. John informs us in Revelation 21:1 that when God has created a "new Heaven and a New Earth...there was no longer any sea." I can't imagine why, but I'm sure that God has His own good reasons.

Yes, praise God, heaven will be a place where our glorified tastebuds will be satiated, and we'll enjoy that "all day singing with *dinner* on the ground."

Part D

"So, What's the Big Deal?"

"Most of us find it very difficult to want 'heaven' at all—except in so far as 'heaven' means meeting again our friends who have died. One reason for this difficulty is that we have not been trained: our education tends to fix our minds on this world."

— C.S.Lewis
Mere Christianity

Chapter
NINETEEN

The Big Deal

C.S. Lewis has stated quite clearly what the "big deal" is: we have not been trained. Thus, as stated in the Prologue, having been personally, grossly ignorant about the particulars of our existence in the third heaven, I first trained myself, by searching the Scriptures, and then I set out to teach others.

As I have spoken through the years with various Christians about heaven, I have discovered many misconceptions. Some think that we become angels, complete with wings and harps. Others believe that we can reappear on earth as ghosts. There is the thought that those in heaven are "watching" us. Then, there are the Roman Catholics who have been taught the non-biblical concept of a place called "purgatory," where their loved ones reside in limbo awaiting justification for their admittance into heaven. This "justification," they are told, only occurs if someone prays and lights enough candles for them. In this manner, their ability to enter heaven is thus presumably accomplished.

Worst of all, some think that everyone eventually goes to heaven. These folks need to realize that the eternal third heaven is the exclusive property of God's children, the elect (Mark 13:27). It is reserved for the redeemed souls of people who have placed their gift of faith and trust in the Person of Jesus Christ and His atoning work on the Cross, and have received Him as Lord and Savior (John 1:12).

Another reason to understand the concept of heaven is this: heaven is where justice ultimately prevails. It is there that we will finally discover the answers to all of the questions previously raised, about the problem of evil in the world—evil that has been permitted by a good and loving God (Isaiah 45:7; Ecclesiastes 7:14).

Heaven is the object of our only hope for true justice. Through the ages, many a child of God has lamented with the psalmist Aseph who wrote, "I envied the arrogant when I saw the prosperity of the wicked. They have no struggles; their bodies are healthy and strong. They are free from the burdens common to man; they are not plagued by human ills. Therefore pride is their necklace; they clothe themselves with violence. From their callous hearts come iniquity; the evil conceits of their minds know no limits. They scoff, and speak with malice; in their arrogance they threaten oppression. Their mouths lay claim to heaven and their tongues take possession of the earth. Therefore their people turn to them and drink up waters in abundance. They say, 'How can God know? Does the Most High have knowledge?' This is what the wicked are like—always carefree, they increase in wealth" (Psalm 73:3-12).

Aseph first described his view of the "happy pagan," then he moved on to his own life; the life of a believer seemed to be less rewarding than that of the infidel.

"Surely in vain have I kept my heart pure; in vain I have washed my hands in innocence. All day long I have been plagued; I have been punished every morning. If I had said, 'I will speak thus,' I would have betrayed your children. When I tried to understand all this, it was oppressive to me till I entered the sanctuary of God; then I understood their final

126

destiny" (Psalm 73:13-17). Aseph had never "understood"justice until he had entered "the sanctuary of God."

It is in "the sanctuary of God," His church, and His word, that we can be trained about heaven and its justice. Unfortunately, that is happening in far too few Sunday school classes. Even if the concepts and realities of heaven are being taught, not enough Christians are availing themselves of the opportunity to learn. That's the "big deal" of this book.

As stated above, heaven is "exclusive"; it is not, all inclusive. In this day and age of multi-culturalism and pluralism, the thought of exclusivity is not politically correct.

The Unitarian Universalist "church," among others, teaches the all inclusive nature of heaven. They have no belief in hell or eternal damnation. In their scheme of things, the final destiny of all humans is heaven. They are partly correct. Everyone will go there, but only God's elect, the chosen few (Matthew 22:14), will stay.

Revelation 22:11-15 paints a very clear picture of the final judgment of all unbelievers. There we read the testimony of John, the apostle, who wrote, "Then I saw a great white throne and Him who was seated on it. Earth and sky fled from His presence, and there was no place for them. And I saw the dead, great and small, standing before the throne, and the books were opened. Another book was opened, which is the book of life. The dead were judged according to what they had done as recorded in the books. The sea gave up the dead that were in it, and death and Hades gave up the dead that were in them, and each person was judged according to what he had done. Then death and Hades were thrown into the lake of fire. The lake of fire is the second death. If anyone's name was not found written in the book of life, he was thrown into the lake of fire."

This was obviously a scene in heaven. John mentions seeing the throne of God. Daniel had a similar vision of God's heavenly throne (Daniel 7:9-10), as did Isaiah (Isaiah 6:1).

John tells us that "earth and sky fled from His presence and there was no place for them" to hide. Is this not a typical picture of fallen man? Remember Adam's initial response to God's presence in the Garden of Eden, after he and Eve had sinned? "He hid from the Lord God among the trees" (Genesis 3:8). Pagans, unregenerates, have been hiding, even running, from God ever since. In Psalm 14:2-3 David writes, "The LORD looks down from heaven on the sons of men to see if there are any who understand, any who seek God. All have turned aside, they have together become corrupt; there is no one who does good, not even one." No human ever seeks God on his own volition. No one is inclined to seek Him until their inclination (Genesis 6:5) has been changed by God (John 6:65).

Now John sees whom these people are: the ones who have always hidden from God. They are "the dead, great and small, standing before the throne." They have been raised from "Hades"—the grave, hell—for their final judgment. They have finally had to appear before God, much to their great consternation, even after their repeated, vain attempts to hide from Him during their earthly lives. They were probably escorted by angels who had plucked them from the grave to stand, *corem deo*—before the face of God. C.S. Lewis said that pagans would be presented before "the face of Him who is the delight or terror of the universe" (*Reflection on the Psalms*). Believers will delight, but pagans will be terrified.

There they stood: former kings, czars, presidents, CEOs, slaves, servants, coolies, ordinary "Joe bag-o-donuts," male and female, Jew and Gentile, black and white, yellow and brown, from every nation, race, and tongue over the face of the whole earth.

They all had one overriding thing in common: they had each refused to believe the truth (II Thessalonians 2:12) and they had exchanged truth of God for a lie (Romans 1:25).

Since the moment of their physical death, they had each been sequestered in Hell (Hades, Sheol). They may have thought that they had already received their final punishment; however, at the "Great White Throne Judgment," they will discover otherwise.

In Isaiah 14:9-11, we read of a conversation, regarding this mind-set, between some departed souls and one other soul whom they are welcoming into Hell.

"The grave below is all astir to meet you at your coming; it rouses the spirits of the departed to greet you—all those who were leaders in the world...all those who were kings over the nations. They will all respond, they will say to you, 'You also have become weak, as we are; you have become like us.' All your pomp has been brought down to the grave, along with the noise of your harps; maggots are spread out beneath you and worms cover you."

These souls that currently reside in hell will one day discover that their present torment cannot be compared with the judgment that is awaiting their appearance before God's throne in the third heaven.

Next, John says, "The books were opened." What are these books and just what information do they contain? What do they have to do with the judgment of unbelievers? What books are sitting there before God's throne? We can only speculate on the answers to those intriguing questions by using other portions of God's Word that speak of this final judgment day.

Certainly, one of these books is the best seller of all times, the most purchased and least read of all books, God's holy Word: the Bible.

There and then, these people will finally be forced to attend a Bible class. They had probably been invited to one that you and I attend, maybe it was in our church, or in a small group meeting at someone's home or local business, but they had either declined the invitation or found it uninteresting, and they never returned. Now, however, they'll truly be a "captive audience." God, the omniscient One, the consummate teacher, will reveal things that they could have learned during their earthly life, things written down by the prophets and apostles, things revealed that God wanted to share with His human creatures.

Another book will contain a record, a log, of the judgments that these people had made about the behavior of others, and yet, had failed to act on for themselves. They may have actually spoken these accusations or, more likely, had merely given thought to them. Regardless, they will be called to give an account of these judgments in the "gospel according to themselves."

In Romans 2:1-3, Paul alludes to this phase of the judgment process: "You, therefore, have no excuse, you who pass judgment on someone else, for at whatever point you judge the other, you are condemning yourself, because you who pass judgment do the same things. Now we know that God's judgment against those who do such things is based on truth. So when you, a mere man, pass judgment on them and yet do the same things, do you think you will escape God's judgment?" God will say to them, "This is what *you said* was right and just and prudent and moral, but you didn't even live up to your own 'standards' of decency."

This time spent, *corem deo*—before the face of God—will also be one of deep soul searching. Things known only to God and those people individually; things they would prefer to remain as secrets will be exposed and judged. "For God will bring every deed into judgment, including the hidden thing, whether it is good or evil" (Ecclesiastes 12:14). The apostle Paul confirms this same notion, as he writes, "God will judge men's secrets through Jesus Christ..." (Romans 2:16).

It has been said that integrity of character is defined by "what you do when you think no one is looking." These people will discover that God has been looking and keeping a record of every seemingly secret thought and deed that they have ever had. In Matthew 10:26 Jesus says, "There is nothing concealed that will not be disclosed or hidden that will not be made known." In Hebrews 4:13 we read, "Nothing in all creation is hidden from God's sight. Everything is uncovered and laid bare before the eyes of Him to whom we must give an account."

A Psalm of Moses speaks also of this final phase of judgment: "You have set our iniquities before you, our secret sins in the light of your presence. All our days pass away under your wrath; we finish our years with a moan" (Psalm 90:8-9).

Thus, another of those open books will contain a record of all of those "secret" sins. Again, it must be said that this final judgment is upon all whom never received the grace of God and salvation in Jesus Christ. The sins of the "redeemed," both secret and overt, have already been judged at the cross of Calvary.

A fourth book will contain a list of their particular sins (Hosea 13:12). This one will be thicker for some than others will. However, if your record book contains only one sin, a single sin that has not yet been covered by the blood of Jesus (Romans 4:7-8), you will stand in this judgment.

Finally, God opens the most vital book of them all: "Another book was opened, which is the book of Life." This is a book that will condemn those standing there, merely because it never mentions any of their names.

"If anyone's name was *not* found written in the book of life, he was thrown into the lake of fire" (Revelation 20:15, emphasis added). "The lake of fire is the second death" (Revelation 20:14).

The lake of fire is a place of loneliness, misery, regret, torment, and, most devastating of all, the absence of God. It is a second death, a spiritual death. For years, these people had told God and God's people, "Leave me alone!" No one that has ever lived has yet experienced life without the presence of God. Even history's most avid atheists never experienced life without God. Up to this point God had always been near them, even after they had died the first death, the physical one, and had gone to Hell (Psalm 139:8). But now they will get their wish; God will leave them alone—terribly, regrettably, and frighteningly alone, for all eternity. During that span of endlessness they will perpetually contemplate their foolish rejection of the truth, and they will long to see those whom they know to be in heaven. It will be a longing never to be satisfied.

Finally, the "big deal" of this book is to give hope to the believer. Heaven is a place that we should be anticipating with great joy. God has promised us that He has prepared great things for us there. In order to look forward to those things, we need to know more about them.

In this world, most of us have experienced the raging "storms of life" in one form or another. Hebrews 6:19 tells us that "we have this hope as an anchor for the soul, firm and secure." The anchor of which the author spoke was a sea anchor. It was like a huge windsock, a canvas like structure that was attached to a rope and tossed out behind the boat in order to give the vessel some stability and enable it to stay the course while the storm raged.

So it is with our hope of heaven. It is an "anchor for the soul," and our security there is firm and certain—if we have received Christ.

Most people, even Christians, fear death. It has been called "the king of terrors" (Job 18:14). Therefore, one of the best reasons for studying the third heaven is to allay this fear and to defeat that horrid "king."

Jesus said, "I tell you the truth, whoever hears my word and believes him who sent me has eternal life and will not be condemned; he has crossed over from death to life" (John 5:24). This means that all believers will simply pass on to heaven, in the very instant when the heart stops. They "cross over from death to life." They go to sleep here and awaken with Jesus in the third heaven. Death is not a period; it's a comma.

Paul tells us that Jesus, having taken our place in death, has utterly "destroyed...the last enemy," death (I Corinthians 15:26).

In his letter to Timothy, Paul encouraged his friend, and us, by saying that Jesus "has destroyed death and has brought life and immortality to light through the gospel" (II Timothy 1:10). The gospel (literally "good news") is God's Word. In order to be enlightened on the issue of "life and immortality," the very subject matter of heaven, we need to study that gospel. We need to learn why our physical death can be considered "good news," not bad.

While it may be perfectly natural, and utterly human, to fear dying (that is, the way in which we will die), there is absolutely no reason for a Christian to fear death itself.

And thus, my friends, "the big deal"!

What we have learned together in the pages of this book has merely abraded the surface of all there is to know about the third heaven. In Deuteronomy 29:29, Moses wrote that, "The secret things belong to the LORD our God, but the things revealed belong to us and to our children forever...."

There are many "secrets things" that remain for us to learn, but those will, of necessity, have to await our entrance into our eternal home. Even the "things revealed" have not been fully disclosed in this book; I would be presumptuous even to suggest that they had. It is hoped, however, that this work will merely serve as a beginning, a stimulus, a springboard, for further personal study of God's Word on these eternal matters. If then, by that studious effort on your part, even more Christians will have attained greater insight into their eternal home, that will truly have become a "big deal."

Epilogue

Final Thoughts

"He who plans for this life, but fails to plan for the next, is wise for a moment but a fool forever."
— C.S. Lewis
God in the Dock

The Prologue began by relating the story of a young man named Barry Colmery, who died in the crash of Swissair flight 111. Since he had been a financial planner, it was quite natural for him to make long term plans—plans that would ensure his family's well being, in the event that he would not live to care for them personally. He dealt regularly with IRAs and pension programs in his business associations, but he also had his own retirement plan, which included life insurance.

Barry went beyond the call of duty when it came to the matter of ensuring a stable future for his twin sons, should he and his wife Julie ever die simultaneously. He had made arrangements, including all of the necessary legal documentation, for his older sister and her husband to raise the boys in the event of a tragedy. It almost seems as though Barry might have read *The Imitation of Christ* by Thomas A. Kempis. In that great Christian classic, we read the following statements on the subject of death: "You won't last long here. Think about what will become of you in another world. You are here today and gone tomorrow; we should plan every word and action as though we were going to die today; the person who thinks about his own death and daily prepares to die will be blessed."

I don't believe that Thomas was speaking here of a morbid preoccupation with death, but, rather, a healthy realization of its inevitability. "Man is destined to die once" (Hebrews 9:27).

Furthermore, Barry had what many of us lack: an eternal perspective. His sense of planning went beyond the temporal. Being a Christian, he had a passion for souls and for reaching his lost friends with the "good news" of Jesus Christ. He cared deeply about the destiny of their eternal souls.

On the morning of his departure for Europe, Barry and his boss Bruce Beard, also a Christian, met for prayer. Part of Barry's request to God on that day was a plea that our Lord would make it possible for all of his fellow workers to gather together at a worship service in our church, sometime after he and Julie had returned from the trip to Europe.

God did answer Barry's request but, undoubtedly, not in the way in which Barry had surely anticipated. One week following the plane crash, our church, The Old North Church of Canfield, Ohio, held a memorial service in honor of Barry, Julie, and their unborn daughter. The sanctuary was filled to overflowing, and the service was also seen on closed circuit television in the fellowship hall. Included in the crowd was every person who had ever worked in Barry's office. That memorial service was truly a worship experience and a tribute to the glory of God. And while Barry and Julie were certainly oblivious to all that transpired there, God was certainly cognizant, and greatly pleased.

Sadly, too few Christians have this eternal perspective that Barry possessed. In his book *No Place For Truth*, David F. Wells posits the reason for this. He says that the process of modernization has dramatically changed our civilization. Americans have lost any sense of permanence and true community. In the early nineteenth century, he reminds us, Americans "had little that was new," while in the twenty-first century,"we have little that has persisted."

We're always looking for the new thing. New designs in clothes; new cars; new jobs; new homes; new "toys"; new uses for the Internet; "new math" (thank God that's over); and there's even something "new" in religion—New Age (though in reality, this is as old as the idolatry of Babylon).

We've lost our sense of the eternal because everything has become so temporary. We are a society that is constantly on the move. We're like nomads, transients, people who hardly get unpacked until we've been uprooted and forced to move on. Even if we do happen to stay in one place for an extended period of time, it has been said of this society that we "unpack everything except our commitments." We desperately need a new perspective on something that never grows old: eternity.

The apostle Paul warned us about becoming too attached to this temporary place called planet Earth when he wrote, "Since, then, you have been raised with Christ, set your hearts on things above, where Christ is seated at the right hand of God. Set your minds on things above, not on earthly things" (Colossians 3:1-2). He also stressed this need for an eternal perspective in his second letter to the church at Corinth when he told them that we Christians should "fix our eyes not on what is seen, but what is unseen. For what is seen is temporary, but what is unseen is eternal" (II Corinthians 4:18).

As a physician, who began the "journey" of the healing art in medical school in 1957, I have witnessed the development of a vast number of new ways to treat illness. In the past forty-three years, there has been a surge of new drugs, new research tools, new surgical techniques, new diagnostic equipment, and, unfortunately, new controls by big government and big business placed on the practice of medicine.

My medical education taught me to care only for the physical and emotional (body and mind) needs of my patients. When I became a Christian and God made me a "new" man (II Corinthians 5:17), He expanded my concerns, beyond the body and mind, to the soul and spirit, to their eternal, and not just their temporal, lives. While never "pushing" my faith on my patients, I always looked for openings to share the concept of eternal life.

This seemed most appropriate, whenever a patient expressed to me a fear of dying. On more than one occasion, my attempts to calm those fears were successful, but the most memorable of all involved a fifty year-old lady with terminal breast cancer. Several days following our conversation on heaven, eternal life, and salvation through Christ, she called to report that her fears were gone and she was now ready to meet God. However, she made one request. "Doctor," she said, "Would you be so kind as to put those encouraging words that you shared with me, on paper, so that others in your practice might receive the hope that I now have?" I promised her that I would, and, as a result, wrote and had printed several thousand copies of the following monograph, entitled *A Matter of Life and Death*. It has been used in nursing homes, hospitals, and in my medical practice for over twenty years. It seems appropriate to close this treatise on the third heaven with this essay.

A Matter of Life and Death

My Dear friend:

I would like to take a few minutes of your time to discuss a most sensitive and urgent matter—a matter of life and death.

You must realize by now that every effort is being expended to control your illness and extend your earthly life. Whether or not your physicians are successful in doing so, remains to be seen, but the very seriousness of your situation makes us contemplate an event that all of us must face sooner or later: our physical death.

Notice that I said "our death," not just yours. Before you finish reading this booklet, I may have already preceded you in death. None of us knows the time or manner in which we will die, but we can know where we will spend eternity. It is that knowledge that takes the fear out of death for me.

Life Seems Unfair

Life has many sources of pleasure and many causes for grief. That's life.

There are numerous things to enjoy and some things to fear. One of the greatest causes of grief and fear, for most people, is the prospect of losing one's life. Yet everyone who has ever been born must eventually face that prospect. It is inevitable. The Bible says, "man is destined to die once" (Hebrews 9:27), but even an atheist knows that.

For some, death comes in the prime of life. That seems unfair. For others, it comes in infancy or childhood before life has even had a chance to start. That too seems unfair. Yet even if we live to a ripe old age, we have to live through years of decreased mobility and productivity, recurring illness, and the loss of friends and loved ones that did not outlive us. The bottom line is that there does not seem to be a convenient or acceptable time to die.

There Is Hope

If death were all we had to look forward to, we would all have great cause for concern. That is not the case however. There is hope. I have hope. Why, you ask, do I have hope? The Bible says, "always be prepared to give an answer to everyone who asks you to give the reason for the hope that you have" (I Peter 3:15). Here is my answer: My hope lies in the person of Jesus Christ. His life, death, and resurrection are facts of history. The apostle Paul told the people of Thessalonica, "Brothers, we do not want you to be ignorant about those who fall asleep, [a biblical term for death] or to grieve like the rest of men, who have no hope. We believe that Jesus died and rose again, and so we believe that God will bring with Jesus those who have fallen asleep in Him" (I Thessalonians 4:13-14).

In another place, Jesus Himself said, "In my Father's house are many rooms; if it were not so I would have told you. I am going there to prepare a place for you. And if I go and prepare a place for you, I will come back and take you to be with me that you also may be where I am" (John 14:2-3).

You probably know where Jesus went: it's heaven. Maybe you don't know how to get there yourself. Read on.

The Gift of Eternal Life

Now when Jesus says that He is going to prepare a place for "you," He is speaking to Christians. These are people who have, by faith, received Him as Lord and Savior. Receiving Him as Savior means that you believe that He died on a cross, in your place, for your sins. The Bible says, "All have sinned and fall short of the glory of God" (Romans 3:23). It also says that "the wages of sin is death, but the gift of God is eternal life in Christ Jesus our Lord" (Romans 6:23). If we accept His death in our place, He saves us from eternal death and gives to us the free gift of eternal life. It is that simple. He has made it simple enough for a child to understand.

Now, you may already believe, in your head, all that I have told you. That's great. It's a start. But head knowledge is not enough. It takes believing and receiving. John tells us, "Yet to all who received Him, to those who believed in His name, He gave the right to become the children of God. Children born not of natural descent, nor of human decision, or a husband's will, but born of God" (John 1:12-13).

All you need do, in order for that to happen, is to ask. Just say, "Lord Jesus, come into my life and take away my sins," and He will. In another place, He promised, "I stand at the door and knock. If anyone hears my voice and opens the door I will come in" (Revelation 3:23).

He is speaking about the door of your heart. Once you invite Him in, He is there to stay. If He is there, you have eternal life. Listen to what the Bible says about that: "God has given us eternal life, and this life is in His Son. He who has the Son has life; he who does not have the Son of God does not have life. I write these things to you who believe in the name of the Son of God so that you may know that you have eternal life" (I John 5:11-13).

Isn't that wonderful? You can *know* that you have eternal life. For years, you have probably heard people say, "You can't know that you will go to heaven when you die." They're wrong. The Bible confirms it. The best-selling book of all time—that has stood the test of time and has outlived all of its critics—says that you can know for sure where you will spend eternity.

Do you see now, why I have hope? I know that I have eternal life because I have the Son—and so can you.

The New Birth

A couple of paragraphs back, the term "born of God" was used. It refers to being born again. That event is described in the third chapter of John when Jesus is visited one night by a very prominent, successful, religious leader by the name of Nicodemus. Jesus immediately recognizes this man's spiritual poverty and tells him that he needs to be born again. Nicodemus doesn't understand, and wants to know how it is possible for a grown man to reenter the womb. Jesus explains that he is confusing physical and spiritual birth.

The first time we are born, we come into the world with a body and a soul. The body, with its five senses, permits us to stay in touch with the physical world around us. The soul, which is the seat of intellect, emotion, personality, and will, allows us to communicate with each other, in those respective contexts.

But man is also a spiritual being. The problem is that our spiritual nature is dormant, or dead, when we are first born. It is by way of our spirit that we are able to communicate with God in prayer, understand His Word, and do His will.

When we are born again, God's Holy Spirit brings our dead spirit to life, and the things of God really begin to make sense. Prior to the new birth, trying to understand God or the Bible is like a blind person trying to appreciate the works of Norman Rockwell or a deaf person the sounds of a symphony.

Growing In Christ

After the new birth has occurred, God's Word comes alive, and the wonderful promises He has written to us become very personal. Listen to this promise: "For God so loved the world that He gave His one and only Son that whoever believes in Him shall not perish, but have eternal life" (John 3:16).

Another promise is equally comforting to the believer: "Whoever believes in the Son has eternal life, but whoever rejects the Son will not see life, for God's wrath remains on him" (John 3:36).

Finally, Jesus said, "I am the resurrection and the life. He who believes in me will live, even though he dies; and whoever lives and believes in me will never die. Do you believe this?" (John 11:25-26)

God's Word is wonderful. In it we find strength, encouragement, and direction. It is our spiritual food, and it is just as important to our spiritual growth as milk, meat, vegetables, and fruit are to our physical growth and well being. You should try to read a little of it every day.

In addition to feeding on God's Word, it is essential to talk with Him each day in prayer. This time of conversation with God, should include expressions of praise and thanksgiving, confession, and asking for His forgiveness (I John 1:9), plus requests made on behalf of others and ourselves.

The Valley of the Shadow

You are facing a tough road. Whether your death comes in the next few weeks or months, or whether you live many more years, when it comes, it will be hard. No one ever promised that death would be easy. But, if you have hope for a bright morning, the night will not seem so long or lonely.

When Billy Graham's mother was dying several years ago, she compared death to the labor of pregnancy. She related that the labor was never a picnic, but that the expectation of the blessed event to follow—the new baby—made the pain and suffering worthwhile. She said that her dying was likewise no picnic, but that the blessed hope of being with her risen Savior Jesus, in heaven, made the pain and suffering more tolerable.

For the Christian, death does not come unattended. God has said, "I will never leave you nor forsake you" (Joshua 1:5).

That includes our time of dying. Psalm 23 reads, "Even though I walk through the valley of the shadow of death, I will fear no evil, for you are with me." Luke chapter 16 tells of a poor beggar, who was carried away by angels to be in the place of other believers. The Bible also teaches, that to be absent from the body is to be present with the Lord.

Jesus promised the thief on the cross next to Him that his faith in Christ had earned him a place in paradise, beginning that very day—the day he died.

You may be wondering what heaven will be like. The Bible gives us glimpses, but does not go into a great amount of detail.

(Note: I had obviously written this booklet before I had studied, in depth, God's revealed truth about heaven.)

Suffice it to say, heaven will be wonderful because it will be spent with Jesus. The Bible does say this, "No eye has seen, no ear has heard, no mind has conceived what God has prepared for those who love Him" (I Corinthians 2:9).

If you're not sure where you will spend eternity, I would suggest that you pray this simple prayer: "Lord Jesus, I'm sorry for my sins. Please forgive me. Come into my heart and help me to live a life that is pleasing to You. Thank You for dying in my place and giving me eternal life. Amen."

It is my prayer that what has been shared in this booklet has caused you to receive Jesus as your Lord and Savior. In closing, I would echo the words of the apostle John, who wrote, toward the end of his gospel, "These are written that you may believe that Jesus is the Christ, the Son of God and that by believing, you may have life in His name" (John 20:31).

Written and given in Love,

Dr. Chuck McGowen

Let's Talk About Heaven
Order Form

Postal orders: 90 Oaktree Lane
Warren, OH 44484

E-mail orders: chmretdoc@aol.com

Please send *Let's Talk About Heaven* to:

Name: _____

Address: _____

City: _____ State: _____

Zip: _____

Telephone: (_____) _____

Book Price: $14.00

Shipping: $3.00 for the first book and $1.00 for each additional book to
cover shipping and handling within US, Canada, and Mexico.
International orders add $6.00 for the first book and $2.00 for
each additional book.

Or order from:
ACW Press
5501 N. 7th. Ave. #502
Phoenix, AZ 85013

(800) 931-BOOK

or contact your local bookstore